Beyond the Code Navigating the AI Frontier Inside

Virtual Horizons in Our Daily Lives

Copyright © 2024 by RK Books

All rights reserved.

No part of this publication may be reproduced, distributed, or transmitted in any form or by any means, including photocopying, recording, or other electronic or mechanical methods, without the prior written permission of the publisher, except in the case of brief quotations embodied in critical reviews and certain other noncommercial uses permitted by copyright law.

This book is a work of fiction. Names, characters, places, and incidents are products of the author's imagination or are used fictitiously. Any resemblance to actual events, locales, or persons, living or dead, is entirely coincidental.

Published by |

Table of Contents

Introduction 1
Chapter 1 Unveiling the AI Frontier 4
    Unveiling the AI Frontier 4
    Exploring Virtual Horizons: The Intersection of Virtual Reality, Augmented Reality, and Mixed Reality 7
Chapter 2 The Rise of Artificial Intelligence 11
    Historical Overview of AI Development 12
    Key Milestones in AI Evolution 14
Chapter 3 Understanding the Code 19
    Deciphering the Fundamentals of AI 20
    Exploring Machine Learning and Neural Networks 22
Chapter 4 AI in Everyday Life 27
    AI in Healthcare: Revolutionizing Patient Care 27
    AI in Education: Transforming Learning Experiences 31
    AI in Finance: Redefining Economic Landscapes 34
Chapter 5 Virtual Assistants: Beyond Convenience 38
    The Role of Virtual Assistants in Modern Society 39
    Ethical Considerations in Virtual Assistant Development 42
Chapter 6 Augmented Reality Bridging the Virtual and Real Worlds 46
    Applications of Augmented Reality in Various Industries 47
    The Future of Augmented Reality Technology 50
Chapter 7 Virtual Reality: Immersive Experiences Beyond 55
    Virtual Reality in Training and Simulation 58
Chapter 8 AI and Personalization 62
    The Power of Personalized Recommendations 63
    Customization and Privacy Concerns 65
Chapter 9 Autonomous Systems: From Self-Driving Cars to Robotics 70
    Advancements in Autonomous Vehicles 71
    Robotics: Enhancing Automation Across Industries 74

Chapter 10 AI and Creativity 78
   AI in Art and Music 79
   The Intersection of AI and Creativity 81
Chapter 11 Ethics and AI: Navigating the Moral Landscape 85
   Ethical Considerations in AI Development and Deployment 86
   Ensuring Transparency and Accountability in AI Development and Deployment 88
Chapter 12 The Future of AI: Opportunities and Challenges 92
   Emerging Trends in AI Research and Development 92
   Addressing Challenges and Shaping the Future of AI 95
Chapter 13 Ethical Frameworks and Guidelines 99
   Introduction to Ethical Frameworks in AI Development 100
   Principles of Ethical AI: Fairness, Transparency, Accountability 104
   Case Studies Ethical Dilemmas and Solutions in AI Deployment 107
   Implementing Ethical Guidelines: Challenges and Best Practices 110
   The Role of Stakeholders: Collaborating for Ethical AI Development 114
Chapter 14 Mitigating Algorithmic Bias: 118
   Understanding Algorithmic Bias and its Implications 118
   Techniques for Detecting and Mitigating Bias in AI Algorithms 122
   Case Studies Addressing Bias in Real-world AI Applications 126
   Promoting Diversity and Inclusivity in AI Research and Development 129
   Strategies for Ensuring Fairness and Equity in AI Deployment 133

Introduction

In the not-so-distant past, the idea of artificial intelligence (AI) seemed like a concept ripped straight from the pages of science fiction novels—a fantastical notion reserved for the realm of imagination and speculation. However, as we stand on the precipice of the 21st century, AI has transcended its fictional origins to become an integral part of our everyday lives. From virtual assistants guiding us through our daily routines to autonomous vehicles navigating our streets, AI has seamlessly woven itself into the fabric of modern society, reshaping the way we live, work, and interact with the world around us.

This book, "Beyond the Code: Navigating the AI Frontier Inside Virtual Horizons in Our Daily Lives," sets out to explore the multifaceted landscape of AI and its profound impact on our lives. It is a journey into the heart of the AI frontier, where virtual horizons beckon us to discover new possibilities and navigate uncharted territories.

At its core, this book is a testament to the remarkable evolution of AI—from its humble beginnings to its current status as a transformative force driving innovation across industries. We will embark on a voyage through time, tracing the historical roots of AI and uncovering the key milestones that have shaped its development. From the groundbreaking discoveries of early pioneers to the cutting-edge technologies of today, we will witness the extraordinary journey of AI as it continues to push the boundaries of what is possible.

But beyond the technological marvels and scientific breakthroughs lies a deeper narrative—one that speaks to the profound impact of

AI on our everyday lives. In the chapters that follow, we will delve into the myriad ways in which AI has infiltrated our daily routines, revolutionizing everything from healthcare and education to finance and entertainment. Through real-world examples and insightful analysis, we will explore the tangible benefits and potential pitfalls of living in an AI-driven world.

Central to our exploration is the concept of virtual horizons—the boundless frontier where the virtual and the real converge to create new realms of possibility. Whether it's through the immersive experiences of virtual reality, the interactive interfaces of augmented reality, or the personalized recommendations of virtual assistants, AI has opened up a world of virtual horizons that transcend the limitations of physical space and time. And as we navigate these virtual horizons, we are faced with both unprecedented opportunities and profound ethical dilemmas that compel us to question the very nature of our humanity.

Indeed, the rise of AI has brought with it a host of ethical considerations that demand our attention and introspection. From concerns about data privacy and algorithmic bias to debates about the future of work and the autonomy of intelligent systems, the ethical implications of AI are vast and complex. As we grapple with these issues, it becomes increasingly clear that the path forward is not always clear-cut, and that the choices we make today will shape the world we inhabit tomorrow.

Yet, amidst the uncertainties and challenges that lie ahead, there is also cause for optimism and hope. For in the midst of this AI revolution, we find ourselves on the brink of a new era of human potential—one where technology serves as a catalyst for positive change and human creativity knows no bounds. As we journey "Beyond the Code" and venture into the AI frontier, let us embrace the virtual horizons that lie before us and chart a course towards a future where innovation, ethics, and humanity converge in harmony.

Chapter 1
Unveiling the AI Frontier

In recent years, artificial intelligence (AI) has transcended its status as a mere buzzword to become a defining feature of the modern era. From virtual assistants anticipating our needs to algorithms powering autonomous vehicles, AI has permeated nearly every aspect of our lives, shaping the way we live, work, and interact with the world around us. This book, "Beyond the Code: Navigating the AI Frontier Inside Virtual Horizons in Our Daily Lives," invites you to embark on a journey into the heart of the AI frontier.

Here, we will explore the remarkable evolution of AI, tracing its origins from speculative concept to practical reality. Through a blend of historical context, real-world examples, and forward-thinking analysis, we will uncover the ways in which AI is reshaping industries, transforming economies, and redefining the very essence of what it means to be human.

As we navigate the virtual horizons of the AI frontier, we will confront complex ethical dilemmas, grapple with profound questions about the nature of intelligence, and envision a future where innovation and humanity intersect in unprecedented ways. Join us as we embark on this journey "Beyond the Code," where the possibilities are as limitless as the virtual horizons that stretch before us.

Unveiling the AI Frontier

In the early 21st century, the world witnessed a technological revolution that would forever alter the course of human history. At the heart of this revolution stood artificial intelligence (AI), a groundbreaking field of computer science aimed at creating intelligent machines capable of performing tasks that traditionally required human intelligence. From humble beginnings as a speculative concept to its current status as a transformative force reshaping society, the journey of AI is one marked by innovation, controversy, and profound implications for the future of humanity.

1. The Genesis of AI From Fiction to Reality

The roots of AI can be traced back to ancient myths and legends, where tales of sentient beings and mechanical marvels captivated the human imagination. However, it wasn't until the 20th century that AI began to take shape as a scientific discipline. Pioneering researchers such as Alan Turing laid the theoretical groundwork for AI with his groundbreaking work on computability and the Turing Test, while early computer scientists like John McCarthy and Marvin Minsky spearheaded efforts to develop AI algorithms and systems. These early endeavors set the stage for the emergence of AI as a bona fide field of study, paving the way for future breakthroughs and innovations.

2. The Evolution of AI: A Timeline of Milestones

Over the decades, AI has undergone a series of revolutions and paradigm shifts, each one bringing us closer to the realization of truly intelligent machines. From the development of expert systems and neural networks to the rise of machine learning and deep learning, the evolution of AI has been marked by a steady progression of advancements and achievements. Key milestones such as the creation of IBM's Deep Blue, which defeated reigning world chess champion Garry Kasparov in 1997, and Google's AlphaGo, which triumphed over top-ranked Go player Lee Sedol in 2016, have demonstrated the remarkable capabilities of AI and its potential to outperform human experts in complex cognitive tasks.

3. AI in the 21st Century: The Rise of the Intelligent Machines

In recent years, AI has experienced a renaissance fueled by exponential advances in computing power, data availability, and algorithmic sophistication. Today, AI-powered technologies permeate nearly every aspect of our lives, from the virtual assistants that help us navigate our daily routines to the autonomous vehicles that promise to revolutionize transportation. The proliferation of AI has led to unprecedented levels of automation and efficiency across industries, driving economic growth, spurring innovation, and transforming the way we work, communicate, and interact with the world around us.

4. The Impact of AI: Transforming Industries and Empowering Lives

The widespread adoption of AI has ushered in a new era of technological innovation, with profound implications for virtually every sector of the global economy. In healthcare, AI-powered diagnostic tools and predictive analytics are revolutionizing patient care, enabling early detection of diseases, personalized treatment plans, and improved clinical outcomes. In education, AI-driven tutoring systems and adaptive learning platforms are providing students with personalized learning experiences tailored to their individual needs and abilities. In finance, AI algorithms are driving algorithmic trading, fraud detection, and risk management, optimizing investment strategies and maximizing returns for investors.

5. The Promise and Peril of AI: Navigating the Ethical Landscape

However, the rapid proliferation of AI has also raised a host of ethical, social, and philosophical questions that demand our attention and introspection. From concerns about algorithmic bias and privacy infringement to fears of job displacement and societal upheaval, the ethical implications of AI are vast and complex. As we entrust intelligent machines with ever-increasing levels of autonomy and decision-making authority, we must grapple with fundamental questions about accountability, transparency, and the moral responsibility of AI developers and users. Moreover, as AI continues to evolve and proliferate, we must confront the possibility of unintended consequences and unforeseen risks, ranging from the erosion of human autonomy and agency to the potential emergence of superintelligent AI systems with capabilities far beyond our comprehension or control.

6. Navigating the AI Frontier: Charting a Course for the Future

As we stand on the cusp of a new era defined by the proliferation of AI, we find ourselves at a crossroads of unprecedented opportunity and profound challenge. The choices we make today will shape the trajectory of AI development and deployment for generations to come, influencing the way we live, work, and interact with intelligent machines. In navigating the AI frontier, we must strive to harness the transformative power of AI for the betterment of humanity, while also mitigating the risks and ensuring that the benefits of AI are shared equitably among all members of society. By embracing a holistic approach to AI governance that prioritizes ethical considerations, human values, and societal well-being, we can chart a course towards a future where AI serves as a force for positive change, enhancing our lives, expanding our capabilities, and enriching our collective experience as human beings.

Exploring Virtual Horizons: The Intersection of Virtual Reality, Augmented Reality, and Mixed Reality

In the digital age, the boundaries between the physical and virtual worlds are becoming increasingly blurred, giving rise to a new frontier of technological innovation known as extended reality (XR). At the forefront of this frontier are three distinct but interconnected technologies: virtual reality (VR), augmented reality (AR), and mixed reality (MR). Collectively, these technologies offer users immersive and interactive experiences that transcend the limitations of traditional media, opening up new possibilities for entertainment, education, communication, and beyond.

1. Virtual Reality (VR) Immersion in the Digital Realm:

Virtual reality (VR) is perhaps the most well-known of the three XR technologies, offering users the ability to immerse themselves in entirely digital environments that are rendered in three dimensions. Through the use of headsets or goggles equipped with motion tracking sensors, users can explore virtual worlds, interact with virtual objects, and even engage with other users in real-time. From immersive gaming experiences that transport players to fantastical realms to virtual tourism applications that allow users to explore far-off destinations from the comfort of their own homes, VR has the potential to revolutionize the way we experience and interact with digital content.

2. Augmented Reality (AR):

Augmented reality (AR) takes a different approach to immersive technology, overlaying digital information and interactive elements onto the user's view of the physical world. Unlike VR, which replaces the user's surroundings with entirely digital environments, AR enhances and supplements the real world with virtual content, creating a blended experience that seamlessly integrates the physical and digital realms. From smartphone apps that superimpose virtual creatures onto the user's surroundings to heads-up displays (HUDs) that provide real-time information about the user's environment, AR has the potential to enhance our perception of reality and transform the way we interact with the world around us.

3. Mixed Reality (MR):

Bridging the Gap Between Virtual and Real Mixed reality (MR) represents the convergence of VR and AR, blending elements of both technologies to create immersive experiences that combine the best of both worlds. In mixed reality environments, virtual objects and digital content are seamlessly integrated into the user's view of the physical world, allowing for interactive and immersive experiences that blur the line between reality and fantasy. Whether it's designing and manipulating 3D models in real-time or collaborating with remote colleagues in virtual meeting spaces, MR has the potential to revolutionize the way we work, learn, and play by providing users with the ability to interact with digital content in a more intuitive and natural way.

4. Applications of Extended Reality (XR) Across Industries:

The potential applications of extended reality (XR) span a wide range of industries and sectors, from entertainment and gaming to healthcare, education, architecture, and beyond. In the entertainment industry, XR technologies are being used to create immersive storytelling experiences that transport audiences to new worlds and perspectives, while in healthcare, they are being leveraged to train medical professionals, simulate surgical procedures, and improve patient outcomes. In education, XR is revolutionizing the way students learn and engage with course material, offering immersive and interactive learning experiences that cater to diverse learning styles and abilities.

5. Challenges and Considerations in the Adoption of XR:

Despite the potential benefits of extended reality (XR) technologies, their widespread adoption faces a number of challenges and considerations. Chief among these is the need for robust hardware and software infrastructure capable of delivering high-quality immersive experiences to users. Additionally, concerns about privacy, security, and data protection must be addressed to ensure that users' personal information is safeguarded and their rights respected. Moreover, as XR technologies become increasingly integrated into our daily lives, it will be important to consider the ethical implications of their use and to ensure that they are deployed in a responsible and equitable manner.

6. The Future of Extended Reality (XR): Opportunities and Beyond:

Looking ahead, the future of extended reality (XR) is filled with promise and potential, as technological advancements continue to push the boundaries of what is possible. From advancements in hardware and software that enable more realistic and immersive experiences to innovations in content creation and distribution that democratize access to XR content, the future of XR is bright and full of possibilities. As XR technologies continue to evolve and mature, they have the potential to transform the way we live, work, and interact with the world around us, ushering in a new era of digital experiences that are more immersive, interactive, and engaging than ever before.

Chapter 2
The Rise of Artificial Intelligence

Chapter 2 delves into the captivating journey of artificial intelligence (AI) from its inception to its current status as a defining force in the modern world. As one of the most revolutionary technological advancements of the 21st century, AI has transformed industries, redefined economies, and reshaped the very fabric of society.

This chapter navigates through the early days of AI research, tracing its origins back to visionary pioneers like Alan Turing, John McCarthy, and Marvin Minsky. We explore the challenges and setbacks faced during the "AI winter" period and the subsequent resurgence fueled by breakthroughs in machine learning and neural networks.

Moreover, we delve into the transformative power of big data and deep learning, which have propelled AI to unprecedented heights of performance and efficiency. However, alongside its remarkable advancements, AI has also sparked profound ethical and societal considerations, prompting discussions about accountability, transparency, and human oversight.

Looking ahead, the chapter examines both the opportunities and challenges that lie on the horizon of AI, emphasizing the importance of responsible AI governance and ethical considerations in shaping a future where AI serves as a catalyst for positive change. Through a comprehensive exploration of the rise of AI, this chapter illuminates the path that has led us to the forefront of the AI revolution.

Historical Overview of AI Development

1. Foundations of AI: The Early Years (1950s-1960s)

The roots of AI can be traced back to the 1950s when researchers began exploring the possibility of creating machines that could exhibit human-like intelligence. In 1950, British mathematician Alan Turing introduced the Turing Test as a measure of a machine's ability to exhibit intelligent behavior indistinguishable from that of a human. Shortly thereafter, in 1956, the term "artificial intelligence" was coined at the Dartmouth Summer Research Project on Artificial Intelligence, often referred to as the birthplace of AI. During this period, researchers focused on symbolic reasoning and problem-solving, laying the groundwork for early AI systems like the Logic Theorist and the General Problem Solver.

2. The AI Winter: Challenges and Setbacks (1970s-1980s):

Despite initial optimism about the potential of AI, the field experienced a downturn in the 1970s and 1980s, known as the "AI winter." Progress in AI research was hampered by limitations in computing power, lack of data, and unrealistic expectations about the capabilities of AI systems. Funding for AI research dried up, leading to a decline in interest and investment in the field. However, despite these challenges, a dedicated community of researchers continued to push the boundaries of AI, laying the groundwork for future advancements.

3. Revival of Interest: Expert Systems and Knowledge-Based Systems (1980s-1990s)

In the 1980s and 1990s, interest in AI was reignited with the development of expert systems and knowledge-based systems. Expert systems were AI programs that used rules and knowledge bases to emulate the decision-making abilities of human experts in specific domains. These systems found applications in fields such as medicine, finance, and engineering, demonstrating the practical potential of AI technologies. Additionally, advancements in machine learning and neural networks laid the groundwork for future breakthroughs in AI research.

4. Rise of Machine Learning and Neural Networks (2000s-Present):

The turn of the 21st century marked a resurgence of interest in AI, fueled by advancements in machine learning, neural networks, and big data. Machine learning algorithms, such as support vector machines (SVM) and decision trees, enabled computers to learn from data and make predictions without explicit programming. Concurrently, researchers began exploring the potential of artificial neural networks—a computational model inspired by the structure and function of the human brain—to solve complex problems and learn from experience. Breakthroughs in deep learning, a subfield of machine learning focused on neural networks with multiple layers of abstraction, revolutionized AI research and paved the way for significant advancements in areas such as image recognition, natural language processing, and speech recognition.

5. AI Applications Across Industries:

Today, AI technologies are being applied across a wide range of industries and sectors, from healthcare and finance to transportation and entertainment. In healthcare, AI-powered diagnostic tools and predictive analytics are revolutionizing patient care, enabling early detection of diseases and personalized treatment plans. In finance, AI algorithms are driving algorithmic trading, fraud detection, and risk management, optimizing investment strategies and maximizing returns for investors. In transportation, AI is powering autonomous vehicles, revolutionizing the way we travel and commute. Additionally, AI is being used in education, agriculture, manufacturing, and many other fields, transforming industries and driving innovation.

6. Ethical Considerations and Future Directions:

As AI technologies continue to advance and proliferate, they raise a host of ethical, social, and philosophical questions that demand our attention and introspection. Concerns about algorithmic bias, privacy infringement, job displacement, and autonomous weapons have sparked debates about the ethical implications of AI and the need for responsible AI development and deployment. Looking ahead, the future of AI holds both promise and challenges. By fostering collaboration, innovation, and responsible AI governance, we can shape a future where AI serves as a force for positive change, empowering individuals, enriching communities, and advancing the collective well-being of society as a whole.

The history of AI development is a testament to human ingenuity, perseverance, and innovation. From its early beginnings as a speculative concept to its current state as a transformative force shaping the world, AI has come a long way. As we continue to push the boundaries of AI research and development, it is essential to remain mindful of the ethical implications and societal impacts of AI technologies, ensuring that they are deployed in a manner that promotes human well-being and societal good.

Key Milestones in AI Evolution

Artificial Intelligence (AI) has undergone a remarkable evolution since its inception, marked by significant breakthroughs, pioneering research, and transformative advancements. This detailed overview will explore key milestones in the development of AI, spanning from its early beginnings to its current state as a ubiquitous and transformative force in society.

1. The Dartmouth Conference (1956): Birth of AI

The Dartmouth Summer Research Project on Artificial Intelligence, held in 1956, is widely regarded as the birthplace of AI. Organized by computer scientist John McCarthy, the conference brought together leading researchers from various fields to explore the possibility of creating machines that could exhibit human-like intelligence. The term "artificial intelligence" was coined at this conference, marking the official beginning of the field.

2. The Logic Theorist (1956): First AI Program

Developed by Allen Newell, J.C. Shaw, and Herbert Simon in 1956, the Logic Theorist was the first AI program capable of solving mathematical problems and proving mathematical theorems. Using a set of predefined rules and logical reasoning, the Logic Theorist demonstrated the potential of AI to perform tasks that were previously thought to require human intelligence.

3. The General Problem Solver (1959): Problem-Solving AI

In 1959, Herbert Simon and Allen Newell introduced the General Problem Solver (GPS), a computer program designed to solve a wide range of problems by simulating human problem-solving techniques. GPS demonstrated the feasibility of creating AI systems capable of reasoning, planning, and problem-solving in diverse domains

4. The Perceptron (1957): Early Neural Network

Developed by Frank Rosenblatt in 1957, the perceptron was one of the earliest attempts to create an artificial neural network. Inspired by the structure and function of biological neurons, the perceptron was capable of learning from experience and adjusting its internal parameters to improve performance. While the perceptron had limitations and fell out of favor in the 1960s, it laid the groundwork for future developments in neural network research.

5. Expert Systems (1970s-1980s): Knowledge-Based AI

In the 1970s and 1980s, researchers began developing expert systems—AI programs that used rules and knowledge bases to emulate the decision-making abilities of human experts in specific domains. Examples include Dendral, a system for chemical analysis, and MYCIN, a system for diagnosing bacterial infections. Expert systems demonstrated the practical potential of AI technologies and found applications in fields such as medicine, finance, and engineering.

6. The AI Winter (1970s-1980s): Setbacks and Challenges

Despite initial optimism about the potential of AI, the field experienced a downturn in the 1970s and 1980s, known as the "AI winter." Progress in AI research was hampered by limitations in computing power, lack of data, and unrealistic expectations about the capabilities of AI systems. Funding for AI research dried up, leading to a decline in interest and investment in the field.

7. Backpropagation Algorithm (1986): Advancement in Neural Network

In 1986, researchers David Rumelhart, Geoffrey Hinton, and Ronald Williams introduced the backpropagation algorithm, a method for training artificial neural networks. Backpropagation revolutionized neural network research by enabling more efficient training of multi-layer networks, overcoming limitations of earlier approaches and paving the way for the resurgence of interest in neural networks.

8. Deep Blue (1997): AI Defeats World Chess Champion

In 1997, IBM's Deep Blue computer defeated reigning world chess champion Garry Kasparov in a highly publicized match. Deep Blue's victory demonstrated the potential of AI to outperform human experts in complex cognitive tasks and sparked widespread interest in AI technologies.

9. AlphaGo (2016): AI Masters the Game of Go

In 2016, Google DeepMind's AlphaGo program achieved a historic milestone by defeating top-ranked Go player Lee Sedol in a five-game match. Go is an ancient board game known for its complexity and strategic depth, making AlphaGo's victory a significant achievement in the field of AI. AlphaGo's success was attributed to its use of deep reinforcement learning and Monte Carlo tree search algorithms.

10. Advancements in Natural Language Processing (NLP)

Recent years have seen significant advancements in natural language processing (NLP), a subfield of AI focused on understanding and generating human language. Breakthroughs such as Google's BERT (Bidirectional Encoder Representations from Transformers) model and OpenAI's GPT (Generative Pre-trained Transformer) models have pushed the boundaries of what AI systems can achieve in tasks such as language translation, sentiment analysis, and text generation

11. Autonomous Vehicles and Robotics

AI technologies have also made significant strides in the fields of autonomous vehicles and robotics. Companies like Tesla, Waymo, and Uber are developing self-driving cars equipped with AI-powered systems for perception, navigation, and decision-making. In robotics, AI algorithms are enabling robots to perform increasingly complex tasks in diverse environments, from manufacturing and logistics to healthcare and exploration.

12. Ethical Considerations and Societal Implications

As AI technologies continue to advance and proliferate, they raise a host of ethical, social, and philosophical questions that demand our attention and introspection. Concerns about algorithmic bias, privacy infringement, job displacement, and autonomous weapons have sparked debates about the ethical implications of AI and the need for responsible AI development and deployment.

13. Future Directions

Looking ahead, the future of AI holds both promise and challenges. By fostering collaboration, innovation, and responsible AI governance, we can shape a future where AI serves as a force for positive change, empowering individuals, enriching communities, and advancing the collective well-being of society as a whole.

Chapter 3

Understanding the Code

Chapter 3 delves into the intricacies of AI algorithms and the underlying principles that govern their operation. As we embark on this exploration, we will uncover the fundamental concepts and methodologies that form the building blocks of artificial intelligence, providing readers with a deeper understanding of the code that powers AI systems.

At the core of AI lies a diverse array of algorithms, each designed to solve specific types of problems and optimize performance in various domains. From classical algorithms like search algorithms and sorting algorithms to modern machine learning algorithms like neural networks and decision trees, the landscape of AI algorithms is vast and multifaceted.

Through a comprehensive examination of these algorithms, we will unravel the mysteries of AI and shed light on the inner workings of intelligent systems. By gaining insight into the principles of AI algorithms, readers will be better equipped to understand, analyze, and evaluate AI technologies in practice.

Moreover, we will explore the ethical implications and societal impacts of AI algorithms, considering questions of fairness, transparency, and accountability in algorithmic decision-making. By fostering a deeper understanding of the code that underpins AI, this chapter aims to empower readers to navigate the complex landscape of artificial intelligence with confidence and clarity.

Deciphering the Fundamentals of AI

Artificial Intelligence (AI) is a complex and multifaceted field that encompasses a wide range of technologies, methodologies, and applications. In this detailed exploration, we will unravel the fundamental concepts and principles that underpin AI, providing readers with a comprehensive understanding of the core elements of this transformative technology.

1. Defining Artificial Intelligence:

At its core, AI is the branch of computer science that aims to create machines capable of performing tasks that typically require human intelligence. These tasks may include reasoning, problem-solving, learning, perception, and language understanding. AI systems are designed to analyze data, extract patterns, make decisions, and adapt to changing environments, often mimicking or augmenting human cognitive abilities.

2. Types of Artificial Intelligence:

AI can be broadly categorized into two main types: Narrow AI and General AI. Narrow AI, also known as Weak AI, refers to AI systems that are designed for specific tasks or domains, such as image recognition, natural language processing, or autonomous driving. General AI, also known as Strong AI or Artificial General Intelligence (AGI), refers to AI systems that possess the ability to understand, learn, and apply knowledge across a wide range of tasks and domains, similar to human intelligence.

3. Machine Learning: The Backbone of AI:

Machine learning is a subfield of AI that focuses on developing algorithms and models that enable computers to learn from data and make predictions or decisions without being explicitly programmed. Supervised learning, unsupervised learning, and reinforcement learning are the three main types of machine learning.

Supervised learning involves training a model on labeled data, unsupervised learning involves training a model on unlabeled data to discover hidden patterns or structures, and reinforcement learning involves training a model to interact with an environment and learn from feedback.

4. Neural Networks: Mimicking the Brain:

Neural networks are computational models inspired by the structure and function of the human brain. They consist of interconnected nodes, or neurons, organized into layers. Each neuron receives input, performs a computation, and produces output, which is passed on to other neurons. Deep learning is a subfield of machine learning that focuses on training deep neural networks with multiple layers of abstraction. Convolutional Neural Networks (CNNs) are commonly used in image recognition tasks, while Recurrent Neural Networks (RNNs) are used in sequential data processing tasks like natural language processing and time series analysis.

5. Natural Language Processing: Understanding Human Language

Natural Language Processing (NLP) is a subfield of AI that focuses on enabling computers to understand, interpret, and generate human language. NLP algorithms analyze and process textual data, extracting meaning, sentiment, and context from written or spoken language. Tasks in NLP include text classification, sentiment analysis, named entity recognition, machine translation, and text generation. Recent advancements in NLP, such as transformer models like BERT and GPT, have significantly improved the performance of AI systems in language-related tasks.

6. Computer Vision: Making Sense of Visual Data

Computer Vision is a subfield of AI that focuses on enabling computers to interpret and analyze visual information from images or videos. Computer vision algorithms detect objects, recognize patterns, and extract features from visual data, enabling applications such as image classification, object detection, facial recognition, and autonomous driving. Convolutional Neural Networks (CNNs) are commonly used in computer vision tasks, allowing AI systems to learn hierarchical representations of visual features.

7. Ethical Considerations and Societal Implications:

As AI technologies continue to advance and proliferate, they raise a host of ethical, social, and philosophical questions that demand our attention and introspection. Concerns about algorithmic bias, privacy infringement, job displacement, and autonomous weapons have sparked debates about the ethical implications of AI and the need for responsible AI development and deployment. It is essential to ensure that AI systems are designed and deployed in a manner that promotes fairness, transparency, accountability, and the protection of human rights.

8. Future Directions:

Looking ahead, the future of AI holds both promise and challenges. By fostering collaboration, innovation, and responsible AI governance, we can shape a future where AI serves as a force for positive change, empowering individuals, enriching communities, and advancing the collective well-being of society as a whole. Continued research and development in AI will lead to new breakthroughs and advancements, enabling AI systems to tackle increasingly complex tasks and domains, from healthcare and education to climate change and sustainability.

Exploring Machine Learning and Neural Networks

1. Understanding Machine Learning:

Machine learning is a subfield of AI that focuses on developing algorithms and models that enable computers to learn from data and make predictions or decisions without being explicitly programmed. The core idea behind machine learning is to train a model on a dataset consisting of input-output pairs, allowing the model to learn patterns and relationships in the data. Once trained, the model can generalize its knowledge to new, unseen data, making predictions or decisions based on learned patterns.

- **Supervised Learning:** In supervised learning, the model is trained on a labeled dataset, where each data point is associated with a corresponding label or output. The goal is to learn a mapping from inputs to outputs, such as classifying images into different categories or predicting the price of a house based on its features.

- **Unsupervised Learning:** In unsupervised learning, the model is trained on an unlabeled dataset, where the goal is to discover hidden patterns or structures in the data. Unsupervised learning tasks include clustering similar data points together or reducing the dimensionality of the data to visualize it in lower-dimensional space.

- **Reinforcement Learning:** In reinforcement learning, the model learns by interacting with an environment and receiving feedback in the form of rewards or penalties. The goal is to learn a policy that maximizes cumulative rewards over time, such as training a robot to navigate a maze or teaching a computer program to play a game.

2. Introduction to Neural Networks:

Neural networks are computational models inspired by the structure and function of the human brain. They consist of interconnected nodes, or neurons, organized into layers. Each neuron receives input, performs a computation, and produces output, which is passed on to other neurons. Neural networks are capable of learning complex patterns and relationships in data, making them powerful tools for a wide range of AI tasks.

- **Feedforward Neural Networks:** Feedforward neural networks consist of layers of neurons arranged in a sequential manner, with each neuron connected to every neuron in the adjacent layers. The input layer receives input data, which is passed through one or more hidden layers before reaching the output layer, which produces the final output. Feedforward neural networks are commonly used in tasks such as classification and regression.

- **Convolutional Neural Networks (CNNs)**: CNNs are a type of neural network designed for processing grid-like data, such as images or audio. They consist of convolutional layers, which apply filters to input data to extract features, followed by pooling layers, which downsample the feature maps to reduce dimensionality. CNNs are widely used in computer vision tasks, such as image classification, object detection, and image segmentation.

- **Recurrent Neural Networks (RNNs):** RNNs are a type of neural network designed for processing sequential data, such as text or time series. They contain recurrent connections that allow information to persist over time, enabling the model to capture temporal dependencies in the data. RNNs are commonly used in tasks such as language modeling, machine translation, and sentiment analysis.

3. Training Neural Networks:

Training a neural network involves optimizing its parameters, such as weights and biases, to minimize a loss function that measures the difference between the predicted outputs and the true outputs. This process, known as backpropagation, involves iteratively adjusting the network's parameters using gradient descent or its variants. During training, the network learns to update its parameters in a way that improves its performance on the training data, allowing it to generalize to new, unseen data.

4. Applications of Machine Learning and Neural Networks:

Machine learning and neural networks have a wide range of applications across various industries and domains. Some notable applications include:

- **Image Recognition:** CNNs are used for tasks such as image classification, object detection, and facial recognition.

- **Natural Language Processing (NLP):** RNNs and transformer models are used for tasks such as machine translation, text summarization, and sentiment analysis.

- **Healthcare:** Machine learning models are used for tasks such as medical image analysis, disease diagnosis, and personalized treatment recommendation

- **Finance:** Machine learning algorithms are used for tasks such as fraud detection, risk assessment, and algorithmic trading.

- **Autonomous Vehicles:** Machine learning models are used for tasks such as object detection, path planning, and decision-making in self-driving cars.

5. Challenges and Future Directions:

While machine learning and neural networks have achieved remarkable success in a wide range of applications, they also face several challenges, such as:

a) **Data Quality:** Machine learning models require large, high-quality datasets for training, which can be difficult to obtain in practice.

Chapter 4

AI in Everyday Life

Chapter 4 delves into the pervasive presence of Artificial Intelligence (AI) in everyday life, exploring its manifold applications that have become integral parts of our daily routines. As AI continues to advance, its impact extends far beyond specialized domains, infiltrating various aspects of modern living, from communication and entertainment to healthcare and transportation.

In this chapter, we embark on a journey to uncover the ways in which AI technologies have seamlessly integrated into our lives, enhancing efficiency, convenience, and productivity. From virtual assistants like Siri and Alexa that streamline our tasks to recommendation systems that personalize our online experiences, AI has become an indispensable companion in the digital age.

Moreover, we examine the transformative role of AI in sectors such as healthcare, where diagnostic algorithms aid in early disease detection, and in transportation, where autonomous vehicles promise to revolutionize mobility. By illuminating the myriad ways in which AI shapes our everyday experiences, this chapter aims to provide readers with a comprehensive understanding of the profound impact of AI on contemporary society.

AI in Healthcare Revolutionizing Patient Care

The integration of Artificial Intelligence (AI) into healthcare represents a monumental advancement in the field, promising to revolutionize patient care in unprecedented ways. From diagnostic accuracy to personalized treatment plans and operational efficiency,

AI is reshaping the healthcare landscape, enhancing outcomes, and improving the overall patient experience. In this comprehensive exploration, we will delve into the multifaceted ways in which AI is transforming patient care, examining its applications across various domains of healthcare.

1. Diagnostic Advancements:

AI-powered diagnostic systems have emerged as powerful tools in the early detection and diagnosis of diseases. By analyzing medical images, pathology slides, and patient data, AI algorithms can accurately identify abnormalities and assist healthcare providers in making timely and informed decisions. For example, in radiology, AI algorithms can detect subtle abnormalities in medical images such as X-rays, MRIs, and CT scans, aiding radiologists in the diagnosis of conditions like cancer, fractures, and neurological disorders. Moreover, AI-driven diagnostic tools can analyze genomic data to identify genetic markers associated with disease risk, enabling early intervention and personalized treatment strategies.

2. Personalized Treatment:

AI enables the development of personalized treatment plans tailored to the unique characteristics and needs of individual patients. By analyzing large datasets of patient data, including genetic information, medical history, and treatment outcomes, AI algorithms can identify patterns and correlations that inform treatment decisions. For instance, AI-powered predictive analytics models can predict patient responses to different treatment options, enabling healthcare providers to select the most effective interventions for each patient. Additionally, AI-driven decision support systems can recommend personalized medication dosages and treatment regimens based on individual patient factors, optimizing therapeutic outcomes and minimizing adverse effects.

3. Predictive Analytics:

AI-driven predictive analytics models are revolutionizing healthcare by enabling the early detection and prevention of adverse health events. By analyzing vast amounts of patient data, including electronic health records (EHRs), wearable device data, and environmental factors, AI algorithms can identify individuals at high risk of developing certain medical conditions and predict future health outcomes. For example, AI-powered predictive analytics tools can identify patients at risk of developing chronic diseases such as diabetes, hypertension, or cardiovascular disease, allowing healthcare providers to intervene early and implement preventive measures to mitigate risk factors and improve health outcomes.

4. Drug Discovery and Development:

AI is transforming the drug discovery and development process by accelerating the identification of novel drug candidates and optimizing the design of clinical trials. AI-driven drug discovery platforms leverage advanced machine learning techniques to analyze biological data, identify potential drug targets, and design new therapeutic compounds with enhanced efficacy and safety profiles. For instance, AI algorithms can analyze molecular structures to predict the binding affinity of drug candidates to target proteins, enabling the identification of promising drug candidates for further preclinical testing. Moreover, AI-powered clinical trial optimization tools can optimize trial designs, patient recruitment strategies, and treatment protocols, accelerating the development and approval of new drugs and therapies.

5. Remote Monitoring and Telemedicine:

AI-powered remote monitoring technologies are revolutionizing healthcare delivery by enabling continuous monitoring of patient health metrics outside of traditional clinical settings. These technologies leverage wearable devices, mobile apps, and telemedicine platforms to collect and analyze real-time data on vital signs, activity levels, medication adherence, and disease progression. For example, AI-driven remote monitoring systems can detect early signs of deterioration in patients with chronic conditions such as heart failure, diabetes, or chronic obstructive pulmonary disease (COPD), allowing healthcare providers to intervene promptly and prevent hospital admissions. Moreover, telemedicine platforms powered by AI algorithms enable virtual consultations, remote diagnosis, and treatment planning, expanding access to care for patients in underserved or remote areas.

6. Operational Efficiency:

AI-driven solutions are optimizing healthcare operations by automating administrative tasks, streamlining workflow processes, and improving resource allocation. AI-powered scheduling systems can optimize appointment scheduling, patient flow management, and resource utilization, reducing wait times, minimizing bottlenecks, and improving the overall patient experience. Additionally, AI-driven predictive maintenance tools can monitor medical equipment performance in real-time, detect potential issues before they occur, and schedule proactive maintenance to minimize downtime and ensure equipment reliability. Furthermore, AI-powered supply chain management platforms can optimize inventory management, procurement, and distribution processes, reducing costs, minimizing waste, and ensuring the availability of essential medical supplies and medications.

7. Ethical Considerations and Challenges:

While AI holds immense potential to revolutionize patient care, it also raises important ethical considerations and challenges. These include concerns about data privacy and security, algorithmic bias and fairness, regulatory compliance, and the impact of AI on the physician-patient relationship. Addressing these ethical considerations is essential to ensuring that AI is deployed in a responsible and equitable manner in healthcare settings. Moreover, healthcare providers must navigate challenges such as data interoperability, integration with existing systems, and the need for specialized training and expertise to effectively implement AI-driven solutions.

AI in Education Transforming Learning Experiences

Artificial Intelligence (AI) is revolutionizing education by transforming traditional learning experiences, enhancing educational outcomes, and empowering both educators and learners. In this comprehensive exploration, we delve into the multifaceted ways in which AI is reshaping education across various domains, from personalized learning and adaptive assessments to administrative efficiency and lifelong learning.

1. Personalized Learning:

AI-powered personalized learning platforms leverage advanced algorithms to tailor educational content and experiences to the individual needs, preferences, and learning styles of each student. By analyzing student performance data, including assessment results, engagement metrics, and learning preferences, AI algorithms can generate personalized learning pathways, recommend relevant instructional resources, and provide targeted feedback and support. For example, adaptive learning systems use data-driven insights to dynamically adjust the pace, difficulty, and content of instruction to optimize learning outcomes for each student, ensuring that they receive the right level of challenge and support to maximize their potential.

2. Adaptive Assessments:

AI-driven adaptive assessment tools enable educators to assess student learning progress, identify areas of strength and weakness, and tailor instruction to meet individual learning needs. These tools use machine learning algorithms to analyze student responses to assessment items, adaptively adjust the difficulty and sequencing of questions, and provide real-time feedback to students and teachers. For instance, adaptive testing platforms can dynamically generate personalized assessments based on each student's proficiency level, ensuring that they are appropriately challenged and engaged. Moreover, AI-powered assessment analytics tools can analyze assessment data to identify patterns and trends, inform instructional decision-making, and measure learning outcomes at both the individual and group levels.

3. Intelligent Tutoring Systems:

AI-driven intelligent tutoring systems provide personalized, adaptive, and interactive support to students as they engage in learning activities. These systems use natural language processing (NLP), machine learning, and cognitive modeling techniques to simulate human tutoring interactions, provide real-time feedback and guidance, and scaffold learning experiences. For example, conversational AI tutors can engage students in interactive dialogues, answer questions, clarify concepts, and provide hints and explanations to support learning. Additionally, AI-powered tutoring systems can track student progress, diagnose learning gaps, and recommend targeted interventions to address areas of difficulty, facilitating mastery learning and promoting academic achievement.

4. Content Creation and Curation:

AI technologies are revolutionizing content creation and curation by automating the process of generating, organizing, and delivering educational resources. Natural language generation (NLG) algorithms can automatically generate educational content, such as text-based explanations, summaries, and quizzes, based on input from subject matter experts or existing educational materials. Content curation platforms powered by AI algorithms can aggregate, categorize, and recommend educational resources, such as articles, videos, and interactive simulations, tailored to the specific needs and interests of educators and learners. Furthermore, AI-driven content recommendation systems can personalize the learning experience by analyzing user preferences, behavior, and performance data to suggest relevant resources and activities that align with their learning goals and interests.

5. Administrative Efficiency:

AI-powered administrative tools are streamlining educational operations and administrative processes, freeing up time and resources for educators to focus on teaching and learning. AI-driven student information systems (SIS) can automate routine administrative tasks, such as enrollment, scheduling, grading, and reporting, reducing administrative burden and increasing efficiency. Additionally, AI-powered chatbots and virtual assistants can provide personalized support and assistance to students, parents, and staff, answering questions, providing information, and facilitating communication and collaboration. Moreover, AI-driven predictive analytics tools can analyze student data to identify at-risk students, predict dropout rates, and inform targeted interventions and support services, enabling proactive student success initiatives and retention strategies.

6. Lifelong Learning:

AI technologies are empowering lifelong learning by providing accessible, personalized, and flexible learning opportunities for learners of all ages and backgrounds. Online learning platforms powered by AI algorithms offer a diverse range of courses, programs, and resources that cater to the diverse learning needs and interests of learners, enabling them to acquire new skills, explore new subjects, and pursue their passions at their own pace and convenience. Moreover, AI-driven personalized learning pathways can recommend relevant courses, learning activities, and resources based on learners' prior knowledge, skills, and goals, facilitating continuous learning and professional development. Additionally, AI-powered adaptive learning systems can provide targeted support and feedback to adult learners, helping them overcome learning barriers and achieve their learning objectives.

AI in Finance Redefining Economic Landscapes

1. Risk Management:

AI-powered risk management systems are enabling financial institutions to identify, assess, and mitigate risks more effectively and efficiently. Machine learning algorithms analyze vast amounts of historical and real-time data to identify patterns, correlations, and anomalies that may indicate potential risks, such as credit defaults, market volatility, or operational failures. For example, AI-driven credit scoring models use alternative data sources and non-traditional variables to assess borrowers' creditworthiness and predict default probabilities more accurately. Moreover, AI-powered risk analytics platforms can simulate complex scenarios, stress test portfolios, and optimize risk-adjusted returns, enabling proactive risk management and decision-making.

2. Trading Strategies:

AI-driven trading strategies are revolutionizing financial markets by leveraging advanced algorithms to identify profitable opportunities, execute trades, and manage portfolios with speed and precision. Machine learning algorithms analyze market data, news sentiment, and social media feeds to identify trends, patterns, and anomalies that may signal trading opportunities. For example, AI-powered trading algorithms can execute high-frequency trades based on real-time market signals, arbitrage price discrepancies across different exchanges, and optimize trading strategies to maximize returns while minimizing risks. Additionally, AI-driven portfolio management systems use predictive analytics and optimization techniques to rebalance portfolios, allocate assets, and hedge risks dynamically, adapting to changing market conditions and investor preferences.

3. Customer Service:

AI-powered customer service solutions are enhancing the customer experience and improving satisfaction levels in the finance industry. Natural language processing (NLP) algorithms enable chatbots and virtual assistants to interact with customers in natural language, answer questions, provide support, and offer personalized recommendations in real-time. For example, AI-driven chatbots can assist customers with account inquiries, transaction disputes, and product recommendations, reducing wait times, improving response rates, and enhancing overall service quality. Moreover, AI-powered sentiment analysis tools can analyze customer feedback, social media posts, and online reviews to identify trends, detect issues, and proactively address customer concerns, fostering customer loyalty and retention.

4. Fraud Detection:

AI-powered fraud detection systems are combating financial fraud by identifying suspicious activities, detecting fraudulent transactions, and preventing unauthorized access to accounts and data. Machine learning algorithms analyze transaction data, user behavior, and network traffic to detect anomalies, outliers, and patterns indicative of fraudulent behavior. For example, AI-driven fraud detection models can flag unusual spending patterns, geographic anomalies, or account takeover attempts in real-time, enabling rapid intervention and mitigation measures. Additionally, AI-powered biometric authentication systems use facial recognition, voice recognition, and behavioral biometrics to verify users' identities and prevent unauthorized access to sensitive information and resources, enhancing security and protecting against identity theft and fraud.

5. Algorithmic Trading:

AI-driven algorithmic trading systems are reshaping financial markets by automating the execution of trading strategies and optimizing trading performance. These systems use machine learning algorithms to analyze market data, historical prices, and order flow to identify trading signals and execute trades with speed and precision. For example, AI-driven trading algorithms can implement quantitative trading strategies, such as statistical arbitrage, trend following, and mean reversion, to exploit market inefficiencies and generate alpha. Moreover, AI-powered execution algorithms can optimize trade execution by minimizing transaction costs, market impact, and slippage, maximizing execution quality and efficiency.

6. Regulatory Compliance:

AI-powered regulatory compliance solutions are helping financial institutions comply with complex and evolving regulatory requirements, such as anti-money laundering (AML), know your customer (KYC), and market surveillance. Machine learning algorithms analyze vast amounts of transaction data, customer records, and market activity to detect suspicious patterns, identify compliance risks, and generate alerts for further investigation. For example, AI-driven AML systems can flag unusual transaction patterns, monitor customer behavior for signs of money laundering or terrorist financing, and generate suspicious activity reports (SARs) to regulatory authorities. Moreover, AI-powered regulatory reporting platforms can automate the generation, validation, and submission of regulatory reports, ensuring accuracy, timeliness, and completeness of regulatory filings.

Chapter 5

Virtual Assistants Beyond Convenience

Chapter 5 explores the transformative role of virtual assistants beyond mere convenience, delving into the profound impact these AI-powered entities have on various aspects of our lives. While virtual assistants like Siri, Alexa, and Google Assistant initially gained popularity for their ability to perform simple tasks and answer questions, their capabilities now extend far beyond mere convenience. In this chapter, we delve into the multifaceted ways in which virtual assistants are reshaping communication, productivity, accessibility, and even emotional support.

Virtual assistants have become indispensable tools in our daily lives, seamlessly integrating into our homes, workplaces, and mobile devices. They have evolved from basic voice-activated interfaces to sophisticated AI-driven platforms capable of understanding context, learning user preferences, and anticipating user needs. Moreover, virtual assistants are increasingly being utilized in specialized domains such as healthcare, education, and customer service, where they offer personalized support, streamline workflows, and enhance user experiences.

Through a comprehensive examination of virtual assistants' capabilities and applications, this chapter aims to highlight their transformative potential in enhancing efficiency, accessibility, and quality of life for individuals and organizations alike. From managing schedules and tasks to providing real-time information and assistance, virtual assistants are empowering users to navigate the complexities of modern life with ease and efficiency.

The Role of Virtual Assistants in Modern Society

In an increasingly digital world, virtual assistants have emerged as integral components of modern society, reshaping the way we communicate, work, and interact with technology. These AI-driven entities, often embodied in voice-activated interfaces or chatbots, have transcended their initial role as mere conveniences to become indispensable tools that streamline daily tasks, provide personalized assistance, and enhance productivity. In this comprehensive exploration, we delve into the multifaceted role of virtual assistants in modern society, examining their impact across various domains and their potential to revolutionize the way we live and work.

1. Communication and Accessibility:

Virtual assistants play a pivotal role in facilitating communication and improving accessibility for individuals with disabilities or impairments. Through natural language processing (NLP) and speech recognition technologies, virtual assistants enable hands-free communication, allowing users to interact with devices and access information using voice commands. For individuals with visual or motor impairments, virtual assistants provide a means of accessing digital content, managing tasks, and navigating the internet more independently. Moreover, virtual assistants can assist users in composing emails, scheduling appointments, and sending text messages, enhancing communication efficiency and accessibility for users of all abilities.

2. Personal Productivity:

Virtual assistants enhance personal productivity by automating routine tasks, managing schedules, and providing real-time assistance to users. Through voice commands or text-based interactions, users can delegate tasks such as setting reminders, creating to-do lists, and managing calendar appointments to virtual assistants, freeing up time and mental bandwidth for more meaningful activities. Moreover, virtual assistants can provide personalized recommendations, such as suggesting relevant articles to read, reminding users of upcoming deadlines, and optimizing daily routines based on user preferences and habits. By serving as virtual productivity coaches, these assistants empower users to stay organized, focused, and productive in both their personal and professional lives.

3. Smart Home Integration:

Virtual assistants are at the forefront of the smart home revolution, serving as central hubs for controlling connected devices, managing home automation systems, and monitoring household activities. Through integration with smart home devices such as thermostats, lights, and security cameras, virtual assistants enable users to control their home environment using voice commands or smartphone apps. For example, users can adjust thermostat settings, dim lights, lock doors, and arm security systems using voice commands issued to virtual assistants like Amazon Alexa or Google Assistant. Moreover, virtual assistants can provide real-time updates on weather conditions, traffic patterns, and news headlines, helping users make informed decisions and stay informed while at home.

4. Educational Support:

Virtual assistants are transforming education by providing personalized learning experiences, facilitating access to educational resources, and assisting students with academic tasks. In the classroom, virtual assistants can serve as interactive teaching aids, delivering instructional content, answering student questions, and providing feedback on assignments. Outside of the classroom, virtual assistants can assist students with homework assignments, research projects, and exam preparation, offering personalized tutoring and support tailored to individual learning needs. Moreover, virtual assistants can recommend educational materials, such as e-books, articles, and videos, based on students' interests, learning preferences, and academic goals, fostering a culture of lifelong learning and intellectual curiosity.

5. Healthcare Assistance:

Virtual assistants are revolutionizing healthcare delivery by providing personalized health information, assisting with medical tasks, and supporting patients in managing chronic conditions. Through integration with healthcare applications and wearable devices, virtual assistants can track vital signs, monitor medication adherence, and provide real-time health reminders to patients. Moreover, virtual assistants can answer health-related questions, provide symptom assessments, and offer general wellness advice, empowering patients to take control of their health and well-being. Additionally, virtual assistants can assist healthcare professionals with administrative tasks, such as scheduling appointments, updating electronic health records, and facilitating telehealth consultations, allowing clinicians to focus more time and attention on patient care.

6. Customer Service and Support:

Virtual assistants are transforming customer service and support by providing personalized assistance, resolving inquiries, and improving overall customer satisfaction. Through chatbots and voice-activated interfaces, virtual assistants can interact with customers in real-time, answering questions, troubleshooting issues, and providing product recommendations. Moreover, virtual assistants can assist with order tracking, delivery updates, and returns processing, streamlining the customer experience and reducing the need for human intervention. By leveraging natural language understanding and machine learning algorithms, virtual assistants can adapt to customer preferences, anticipate needs, and deliver tailored support across multiple channels, including websites, mobile apps, and social media platforms.

7. Ethical and Privacy Considerations:

While virtual assistants offer numerous benefits and conveniences, their widespread adoption raises important ethical and privacy considerations. Concerns have been raised about data privacy, security breaches, and the potential for misuse or abuse of personal information collected by virtual assistants. Moreover, there are questions about the transparency of data collection practices, the use of user data for targeted advertising, and the potential for algorithmic bias or discrimination in virtual assistant interactions. Addressing these ethical and privacy concerns is essential to ensuring that virtual assistants are deployed in a responsible and ethical manner, respecting user privacy rights and promoting trust and transparency in virtual assistant interactions.

Ethical Considerations in Virtual Assistant Development

As virtual assistants continue to proliferate across various domains, from smartphones and smart speakers to customer service and healthcare, it becomes increasingly crucial to address the ethical implications associated with their development, deployment, and usage. While virtual assistants offer convenience, efficiency, and personalized assistance, they also raise significant ethical concerns related to privacy, security, bias, autonomy, and transparency. In this comprehensive exploration, we delve into the ethical considerations surrounding virtual assistant development, examining the challenges they present and proposing strategies to mitigate potential risks and promote responsible AI usage.

1. Privacy and Data Security:

One of the foremost ethical considerations in virtual assistant development is privacy protection and data security. Virtual assistants collect vast amounts of user data, including voice recordings, personal preferences, location information, and search history, to provide personalized assistance and improve user experiences. However, the collection, storage, and processing of such sensitive data raise concerns about user privacy, consent, and data security. Developers must implement robust encryption protocols, data anonymization techniques, and access controls to safeguard user data from unauthorized access, breaches, and misuse. Moreover, transparent privacy policies, user consent mechanisms, and opt-out options should be provided to users to empower them to make informed choices about the collection and use of their personal information.

2. Bias and Fairness:

Another critical ethical consideration in virtual assistant development is the mitigation of bias and promotion of fairness in AI algorithms and decision-making processes. Virtual assistants rely on machine learning algorithms trained on vast datasets, which may contain biased or incomplete information, leading to biased outcomes and discriminatory behavior. Developers must implement measures to identify, mitigate, and prevent bias in AI systems, such as data preprocessing techniques, algorithmic transparency, and fairness-aware machine learning models. Moreover, diversity and inclusion should be prioritized in dataset collection and model training to ensure that virtual assistants represent diverse perspectives and mitigate algorithmic biases that disproportionately affect marginalized communities

3. Autonomy and Agency:

Virtual assistants raise ethical concerns related to user autonomy and agency, particularly regarding the delegation of decision-making authority to AI systems. Users may rely heavily on virtual assistants to make decisions, perform tasks, and manage their daily lives, potentially eroding their autonomy and decision-making capabilities. Developers must strike a balance between empowering users with personalized assistance and preserving their autonomy and agency. Virtual assistants should offer transparent explanations, options, and opportunities for user input, allowing users to maintain control over their interactions and decisions. Moreover, users should have the ability to override virtual assistant recommendations, adjust settings, and customize preferences to align with their individual values and preferences.

4. Transparency and Accountability:

Transparency and accountability are essential principles in virtual assistant development to ensure that AI systems are transparent, explainable, and accountable for their actions and decisions. Users should be provided with clear information about how virtual assistants work, what data they collect, and how that data is used to inform recommendations and actions. Moreover, virtual assistants should offer explanations for their decisions, disclose potential limitations or biases, and provide avenues for users to seek clarification or raise concerns. Developers must also establish mechanisms for accountability and oversight to address instances of algorithmic errors, misconduct, or misuse, such as regular audits, independent reviews, and user feedback mechanisms.

5. User Consent and Control:

User consent and control are fundamental ethical considerations in virtual assistant development, as users should have the autonomy to choose whether and how they interact with AI systems and control the collection and use of their personal data. Developers must obtain explicit consent from users before collecting, storing, or processing their personal information and provide clear options for users to opt out or limit the scope of data collection. Moreover, users should have granular control over their privacy settings, preferences, and permissions, allowing them to adjust privacy settings, delete data, and manage access rights as needed. Virtual assistants should also offer transparent mechanisms for users to revoke consent, access their data, and request its deletion or anonymization.

6. Human-AI Interaction and Empathy:

Human-AI interaction raises ethical considerations related to empathy, trust, and emotional well-being, as virtual assistants increasingly engage in emotionally charged interactions with users. While virtual assistants are designed to simulate human-like interactions and provide empathetic responses, they lack genuine emotions, intentions, and understanding. Developers must be mindful of the emotional impact of virtual assistant interactions on users and design AI systems that prioritize empathy, compassion, and ethical behavior. Virtual assistants should be trained to recognize and respond to emotional cues appropriately, provide empathetic support and encouragement, and refer users to human experts or resources when necessary

7. Continual Learning and Improvement:

Virtual assistants require continual learning and improvement to adapt to evolving user needs, preferences, and expectations and deliver personalized, relevant, and accurate assistance. However, continual learning raises ethical concerns related to data privacy, model bias, and unintended consequences. Developers must implement safeguards to ensure that virtual assistants learn from diverse and representative data sources, receive ongoing training and feedback, and adapt their behavior in accordance with ethical guidelines and principles. Moreover, virtual assistants should be capable of recognizing and correcting errors, biases, and misinformation, fostering user trust and confidence in AI systems over time.

Chapter 6
Augmented Reality Bridging the Virtual and Real Worlds

Chapter 6 explores the fascinating realm of augmented reality (AR) and its transformative impact on bridging the virtual and real worlds. Augmented reality technology overlays digital content and virtual objects onto the physical environment, blurring the boundaries between the digital and physical realms and enhancing our perception of reality. In this chapter, we delve into the multifaceted applications of augmented reality across various domains, from entertainment and gaming to education, healthcare, and enterprise.

Augmented reality has evolved from a novelty to a powerful tool that enhances experiences, fosters creativity, and improves productivity in diverse contexts. By seamlessly integrating digital information and virtual elements into the physical world, augmented reality enables users to interact with their surroundings in new and immersive ways. From interactive museum exhibits and virtual try-on experiences to medical simulations and industrial training applications, augmented reality is revolutionizing how we learn, work, and interact with the world around us.

Through real-world examples, case studies, and emerging trends, this chapter explores the transformative potential of augmented reality in reshaping human experiences, fostering innovation, and unlocking new opportunities for exploration and discovery. As augmented reality continues to advance and evolve, it holds the promise of revolutionizing how we perceive and interact with the world, blurring the lines between imagination and reality in unprecedented ways.

Applications of Augmented Reality in Various Industries

Augmented Reality (AR) has emerged as a transformative technology with the potential to revolutionize numerous industries by overlaying digital information and virtual objects onto the physical world, enhancing user experiences and driving innovation. From retail and healthcare to education, manufacturing, and entertainment, AR offers a wide range of applications that improve productivity, efficiency, and engagement across diverse sectors. In this comprehensive exploration, we delve into the multifaceted applications of augmented reality in various industries, examining how this technology is reshaping processes, workflows, and customer interactions to unlock new opportunities and deliver value.

1. Retail and E-Commerce:

In the retail and e-commerce industry, augmented reality is transforming the way consumers shop by providing immersive and interactive experiences that bridge the gap between online and offline retail environments. AR-enabled virtual try-on experiences allow customers to visualize products, such as clothing, accessories, and cosmetics, in real-time using their smartphones or AR-enabled devices, helping them make more informed purchasing decisions and reducing returns. Moreover, AR-powered product visualization tools enable retailers to create virtual showrooms and interactive product displays that showcase their offerings in a compelling and engaging manner, enhancing the online shopping experience and driving sales.

2. Healthcare and Medical Training:

Augmented reality is revolutionizing healthcare and medical training by providing immersive simulations, virtual anatomy models, and surgical planning tools that enhance education, training, and patient care. Medical students and professionals can use AR applications to visualize complex anatomical structures, simulate surgical procedures, and practice medical interventions in a risk-free environment, improving learning outcomes and proficiency. Moreover, AR-powered medical imaging tools enable clinicians to overlay diagnostic images, such as MRI scans and CT scans, onto patients' bodies during surgical planning and procedures, enhancing precision, accuracy, and patient safety.

3. Education and Training:

Augmented reality is enhancing education and training by providing immersive learning experiences, interactive simulations, and virtual field trips that engage students and promote deeper understanding of complex concepts. AR applications in education enable students to interact with digital content overlaid onto physical objects, such as textbooks, posters, and educational materials, bringing lessons to life and catering to diverse learning styles. Moreover, AR-powered training simulations offer hands-on learning opportunities for vocational skills, technical training, and professional development, allowing learners to practice tasks and procedures in a realistic and interactive environment, fostering skill acquisition and retention.

4. Architecture and Construction:

In the architecture and construction industry, augmented reality is revolutionizing design visualization, project planning, and on-site collaboration by providing architects, engineers, and construction professionals with real-time access to digital models, plans, and information overlaid onto physical spaces. AR-enabled design visualization tools allow stakeholders to visualize architectural designs, building plans, and interior layouts in the context of the actual construction site, facilitating design reviews, stakeholder engagement, and decision-making. Moreover, AR-powered on-site assistance tools provide construction workers with step-by-step instructions, safety guidelines, and real-time feedback overlaid onto equipment and machinery, improving productivity, efficiency, and safety on construction sites.

5. Manufacturing and Maintenance:

Augmented reality is enhancing manufacturing and maintenance operations by providing technicians and operators with real-time access to digital instructions, schematics, and diagnostic data overlaid onto machinery, equipment, and industrial environments. AR-enabled maintenance and repair tools offer on-the-job guidance, troubleshooting assistance, and interactive manuals that help technicians diagnose problems, perform repairs, and conduct preventive maintenance tasks more efficiently. Moreover, AR-powered training simulations and on-the-job support tools improve workforce training, skills development, and knowledge transfer, reducing downtime, improving productivity, and ensuring operational continuity in manufacturing facilities.

6. Entertainment and Gaming:

In the entertainment and gaming industry, augmented reality is creating immersive gaming experiences, interactive storytelling opportunities, and location-based entertainment attractions that blur the boundaries between the virtual and physical worlds. AR-enabled mobile games allow players to interact with virtual characters, objects, and environments overlaid onto the real-world surroundings, transforming everyday locations into game worlds and encouraging social interaction and exploration. Moreover, AR-powered storytelling experiences, such as immersive theater productions and interactive art installations, engage audiences in new and innovative ways, blurring the lines between fiction and reality and pushing the boundaries of creative expression.

The Future of Augmented Reality Technology

Augmented Reality (AR) has emerged as a transformative technology with the potential to revolutionize how we interact with the world around us. By overlaying digital information and virtual objects onto the physical environment, AR enhances our perception of reality, offering immersive and interactive experiences across diverse domains. As AR technology continues to evolve and mature, it is poised to reshape numerous industries, from entertainment and gaming to healthcare, education, and enterprise. In this comprehensive exploration, we delve into the future of augmented reality technology, examining emerging trends, challenges, and opportunities that will shape its evolution in the years to come.

1. Advancements in Hardware:

One of the key drivers of the future of AR technology is advancements in hardware, including headsets, smart glasses, and mobile devices. As technology companies invest in research and development, we can expect to see the emergence of more compact, lightweight, and ergonomic AR devices with improved display quality, field of view, and battery life. Moreover, innovations in sensor technology, such as depth-sensing cameras and LiDAR sensors, will enable more accurate and responsive AR experiences, enhancing object recognition, spatial mapping, and gesture tracking capabilities.

2. Integration with 5G Networks:

The rollout of 5G networks is set to accelerate the adoption of AR technology by providing high-speed, low-latency connectivity that enables seamless streaming of immersive content and real-time collaboration. With 5G-enabled AR devices, users will be able to access and interact with high-definition AR experiences, such as live streaming of augmented reality events, multiplayer gaming, and remote assistance applications, without experiencing buffering or lag. Moreover, 5G networks will enable edge computing capabilities that offload processing tasks to cloud servers, enabling more complex and resource-intensive AR applications.

3. Advancements in Computer Vision:

Advances in computer vision algorithms and machine learning techniques are driving the development of more intelligent and context-aware AR experiences. Future AR systems will be capable of recognizing and understanding complex scenes, objects, and gestures in real-time, enabling more natural and intuitive interactions with virtual content. Moreover, deep learning algorithms will enable AR devices to adapt to users' preferences, behaviors, and environments, personalizing content and recommendations to enhance user engagement and satisfaction.

4. Spatial Computing:

Spatial computing is poised to revolutionize AR technology by enabling more immersive and interactive experiences that seamlessly blend virtual and physical elements in three-dimensional space. With advancements in spatial mapping, object recognition, and scene understanding, AR devices will be able to create persistent digital overlays that persistently align with the physical environment, enabling users to interact with virtual objects as if they were part of the real world. Moreover, spatial computing will enable multi-user AR experiences, allowing multiple users to collaborate, communicate, and interact with shared virtual content in real-time.

5. AI-driven Content Creation:

AI-driven content creation tools will democratize AR development by enabling creators and developers to generate high-quality AR content more easily and efficiently. Future AR platforms will leverage AI algorithms to automate tasks such as 3D modeling, texture mapping, and animation, reducing the time and expertise required to create immersive AR experiences. Moreover, AI-powered content recommendation systems will analyze user preferences, behavior, and context to deliver personalized AR content and recommendations that align with users' interests and objectives.

6. Integration with IoT and Wearables:

The integration of AR technology with Internet of Things (IoT) devices and wearables will enable more seamless and context-aware experiences that enhance productivity, safety, and convenience. AR-enabled IoT devices, such as smart home appliances, industrial sensors, and connected vehicles, will provide real-time feedback and notifications overlaid onto the physical environment, enabling users to monitor and control connected devices more intuitively. Moreover, AR-enabled wearables, such as smart glasses and head-mounted displays, will provide hands-free access to information, navigation, and communication, empowering users to stay connected and informed while on the go.

7. Applications in Healthcare and Medicine:

In the healthcare and medicine sector, AR technology holds the promise of revolutionizing patient care, medical training, and surgical procedures. Future AR-enabled medical devices will provide clinicians with real-time access to patient data, diagnostic images, and treatment plans overlaid onto the surgical field, enhancing precision, accuracy, and patient safety during procedures. Moreover, AR-powered medical training simulations will enable students and professionals to practice surgical techniques, medical interventions, and patient care scenarios in immersive and realistic environments, improving learning outcomes and proficiency.

8. Enhanced Remote Collaboration:

Augmented reality technology will facilitate enhanced remote collaboration by enabling users to interact with virtual content and share experiences in real-time regardless of their physical location. Future AR collaboration platforms will enable users to participate in virtual meetings, presentations, and design reviews using AR-enabled devices, allowing participants to visualize and manipulate 3D models, annotate digital content, and communicate with gestures and voice commands. Moreover, AR-powered remote assistance applications will enable experts to provide real-time guidance and support to field technicians, maintenance workers, and remote teams, reducing downtime and improving productivity.

9. Expansion of AR in Education:

Augmented reality technology will play an increasingly prominent role in education by providing immersive and interactive learning experiences that engage students and foster deeper understanding of complex concepts. Future AR-enabled educational content will enable students to explore virtual environments, conduct virtual experiments, and interact with digital simulations that bring abstract concepts to life. Moreover, AR-powered adaptive learning systems will personalize instruction and assessment based on students' individual needs, preferences, and learning styles, enabling more effective and personalized learning experiences.

10. Ethical and Privacy Considerations:

As augmented reality technology becomes more pervasive and immersive, it will raise important ethical and privacy considerations that must be addressed to ensure responsible and ethical use. Developers and policymakers must prioritize user privacy, data security, and transparency in AR applications, implementing robust data protection measures, user consent mechanisms, and privacy-by-design principles to safeguard user rights and mitigate potential risks. Moreover, stakeholders must address concerns related to digital privacy, augmented surveillance, and the potential for misuse

Chapter 7

Virtual Reality Immersive Experiences Beyond

Chapter 7 delves into the captivating realm of Virtual Reality (VR) and its transformative potential to create immersive experiences that transcend the boundaries of physical reality. Virtual Reality technology immerses users in computer-generated environments, allowing them to interact with digital content and simulated worlds in a highly immersive and realistic manner. From entertainment and gaming to education, healthcare, and beyond, VR offers a multitude of applications that redefine how we experience and interact with digital content. In this chapter, we explore the evolution of Virtual Reality technology, its current state of the art, and the emerging trends that are shaping its future.

As VR technology continues to advance and become more accessible, it holds the promise of revolutionizing numerous industries and unlocking new possibilities for creativity, innovation, and human expression. From virtual travel and social interaction to training simulations and therapeutic applications, VR has the potential to transform how we learn, work, play, and connect with others in ways previously unimaginable. Through a comprehensive examination of VR's capabilities and applications, this chapter aims to provide insights into the profound impact of Virtual Reality on our lives and the exciting opportunities that lie ahead in the immersive world of VR experiences and beyond.

Virtual Reality (VR) has revolutionized the entertainment and gaming industry by offering immersive experiences that transport users into digital worlds and interactive narratives. Unlike traditional forms of entertainment, VR allows users to actively engage with virtual environments, characters, and scenarios, blurring the lines between fiction and reality. In this comprehensive exploration, we delve into the diverse applications of Virtual Reality in entertainment and gaming, examining how this transformative technology has reshaped storytelling, gaming experiences, and interactive content creation.

1. Immersive Storytelling:

Virtual Reality has redefined storytelling by enabling creators to immerse audiences in compelling narratives and interactive experiences. VR storytelling transcends traditional mediums by allowing users to become active participants in the narrative, influencing the storyline, and shaping the outcome through their actions and choices. Whether it's exploring fantastical worlds, solving mysteries, or experiencing historical events firsthand, VR storytelling offers unparalleled levels of immersion and engagement. Creators leverage immersive technologies such as 360-degree videos, spatial audio, and interactive branching narratives to create immersive experiences that captivate and resonate with audiences on a visceral level.

2. Immersive Gaming Experiences:

VR gaming has transformed the gaming industry by providing players with immersive and interactive experiences that transcend traditional gaming conventions. In VR games, players can physically move within virtual environments, interact with objects, and engage with virtual characters in ways that were previously impossible. Whether it's exploring vast open worlds, engaging in adrenaline-pumping action sequences, or solving puzzles in immersive escape rooms, VR gaming offers a level of immersion and presence that transports players to new realities. Developers leverage VR hardware such as headsets, motion controllers, and haptic feedback devices to create immersive gaming experiences that blur the boundaries between the physical and virtual worlds.

3. Social VR Experiences:

Virtual Reality has revolutionized social interaction by enabling users to connect and interact with others in immersive virtual environments. Social VR platforms allow users to meet up with friends, attend virtual events, and engage in shared activities in virtual spaces that replicate real-world environments or fantastical landscapes. Whether it's hanging out with friends in virtual living rooms, attending virtual concerts and events, or exploring virtual worlds together, Social VR experiences facilitate meaningful connections and interactions in ways that transcend physical boundaries. Developers leverage VR technologies such as avatars, spatial audio, and shared experiences to create immersive social environments that foster collaboration, communication, and community building.

4. Immersive Cinematic Experiences:

Virtual Reality has revolutionized the way we experience cinematic content by providing immersive and interactive experiences that transport viewers into the heart of the action. VR cinematic experiences allow users to step inside movies, documentaries, and immersive narratives, where they can explore scenes from different perspectives, interact with characters, and influence the storyline through their actions. Whether it's experiencing the thrill of a roller coaster ride, diving into the depths of the ocean, or exploring distant planets in outer space, VR cinematic experiences offer a level of immersion and presence that traditional media cannot replicate. Creators leverage VR technologies such as volumetric capture, spatial audio, and interactive storytelling to create cinematic experiences that engage and captivate audiences in new and exciting ways.

5. Immersive Theme Park Attractions:

Virtual Reality has transformed the theme park industry by offering immersive and interactive attractions that combine physical rides with virtual experiences. VR theme park attractions allow visitors to embark on thrilling adventures, engage in epic battles, and explore fantastical worlds while riding roller coasters, simulators, and other motion-based rides. Whether it's battling alien invaders, racing through futuristic cityscapes, or exploring ancient ruins, VR theme park attractions offer a level of immersion and excitement that traditional rides cannot match. Theme parks leverage VR technologies such as motion tracking, synchronized motion platforms, and multi-sensory effects to create immersive experiences that thrill and delight visitors of all ages

Virtual Reality in Training and Simulation

Virtual Reality (VR) has emerged as a powerful tool for training and simulation across various industries, offering immersive and interactive experiences that replicate real-world scenarios in a safe and controlled environment. From military and aviation to healthcare, manufacturing, and beyond, VR training and simulation applications provide learners with hands-on experience, procedural practice, and skill development opportunities that enhance learning outcomes and improve performance. In this comprehensive exploration, we delve into the diverse applications of Virtual Reality in training and simulation, examining how this transformative technology is revolutionizing workforce development, skill acquisition, and professional training

1. Military Training:

Virtual Reality has revolutionized military training by providing soldiers with realistic and immersive simulations of combat scenarios, tactical maneuvers, and mission-critical tasks. VR training simulations enable soldiers to practice skills such as weapon handling, squad tactics, and battlefield communication in a safe and controlled environment, preparing them for real-world missions and deployments. Moreover, VR training allows military personnel to experience high-stress situations and decision-making challenges, enhancing their ability to perform under pressure and adapt to rapidly changing circumstances on the battlefield.

2. Aviation Training:

Virtual Reality has transformed aviation training by providing pilots with realistic flight simulations, cockpit familiarization, and emergency procedures training. VR flight simulators allow pilots to practice maneuvers, instrument procedures, and emergency protocols in a highly immersive and interactive environment, without the need for expensive aircraft or flight hours. Moreover, VR training simulations can replicate a wide range of weather conditions, aircraft malfunctions, and operational scenarios, enabling pilots to develop proficiency and confidence in handling various situations they may encounter during flight.

3. Healthcare Training:

Virtual Reality has revolutionized healthcare training by providing medical professionals with realistic simulations of medical procedures, surgical interventions, and patient care scenarios. VR medical simulations allow students and practitioners to practice skills such as surgical techniques, patient assessment, and medical interventions in a risk-free and controlled environment, reducing the need for expensive cadaver labs or live-patient training. Moreover, VR training simulations can replicate complex medical conditions, anatomical variations, and surgical complications, enabling healthcare professionals to develop expertise and proficiency in treating a wide range of patient cases.

4. Manufacturing Training:

Virtual Reality has transformed manufacturing training by providing workers with immersive simulations of equipment operation, assembly processes, and maintenance procedures. VR manufacturing simulations allow trainees to practice tasks such as equipment setup, tool operation, and quality control in a virtual factory environment, without the need for physical machinery or production lines. Moreover, VR training simulations can simulate hazardous or high-risk scenarios, such as equipment malfunctions or safety incidents, allowing workers to develop safety awareness and emergency response skills in a safe and controlled setting.

5. Emergency Response Training:

Virtual Reality has revolutionized emergency response training by providing first responders with realistic simulations of disaster scenarios, rescue operations, and medical emergencies. VR emergency response simulations allow firefighters, paramedics, and law enforcement officers to practice skills such as incident command, triage, and patient care in immersive and high-stress environments, without the need for real-world emergencies. Moreover, VR training simulations can replicate dynamic and unpredictable situations, such as building collapses or natural disasters, enabling responders to develop teamwork, communication, and decision-making skills under pressure.

6. Customer Service Training:

Virtual Reality has transformed customer service training by providing employees with realistic simulations of customer interactions, sales scenarios, and service encounters. VR customer service simulations allow trainees to practice skills such as active listening, conflict resolution, and product demonstrations in a virtual retail or hospitality environment, without the need for real customers or physical stores. Moreover, VR training simulations can simulate challenging or high-pressure situations, such as handling irate customers or managing busy queues, allowing employees to develop empathy, resilience, and communication skills in a safe and controlled setting.

7. Soft Skills Training:

Virtual Reality has revolutionized soft skills training by providing learners with immersive simulations of interpersonal communication, leadership, and teamwork scenarios. VR soft skills simulations allow trainees to practice skills such as effective communication, negotiation, and collaboration in virtual work environments, without the need for real colleagues or face-to-face interactions. Moreover, VR training simulations can simulate diverse and inclusive workplace scenarios, enabling learners to develop cultural awareness, empathy, and diversity skills in a safe and supportive setting.

8. Educational Training:

Virtual Reality has transformed educational training by providing students with immersive simulations of educational concepts, scientific phenomena, and historical events. VR educational simulations allow learners to explore virtual environments, conduct experiments, and interact with digital content in ways that enhance learning engagement and retention. Moreover, VR training simulations can cater to diverse learning styles and preferences, enabling students to learn at their own pace and receive personalized feedback and guidance from virtual tutors or instructors.

Chapter 8
AI and Personalization

In Chapter 8, we explore the dynamic synergy between Artificial Intelligence (AI) and personalization, delving into how AI-driven technologies have revolutionized the landscape of customer engagement. Personalization, once a mere buzzword, has become a cornerstone of modern business strategies, enabled by the powerful capabilities of AI algorithms. This chapter illuminates how businesses harness the predictive prowess of AI to tailor customer experiences with unparalleled precision, navigating the intricacies of individual preferences, behaviors, and contexts.

Through AI, businesses can decipher vast troves of data, unveiling insights that unveil the intricacies of customer behavior, preferences, and intents. From predictive analytics to dynamic content personalization, AI-driven solutions empower businesses to craft bespoke interactions across various touchpoints, amplifying customer satisfaction, loyalty, and retention. Moreover, AI augments customer support, marketing campaigns, and product recommendations, fostering deeper connections and driving sustainable growth.

However, as AI and personalization intertwine, ethical considerations surrounding data privacy and algorithmic bias come to the forefront. This chapter navigates the ethical implications of AI-driven personalization, underscoring the importance of transparent data practices and algorithmic fairness in fostering trust and accountability. Through this exploration, readers gain insight into the transformative potential of AI-powered personalization and the imperative of ethical stewardship in shaping the future of customer engagement.

The Power of Personalized Recommendations

In the era of digital abundance, consumers are inundated with an overwhelming array of choices across various products and services. Amidst this abundance, personalized recommendations stand out as a beacon of guidance, helping consumers navigate the vast landscape of options to find products and content that resonate with their preferences and interests. Powered by advanced algorithms and machine learning techniques, personalized recommendations have transformed the way businesses engage with consumers, driving sales, enhancing user experiences, and fostering long-term loyalty. In this comprehensive exploration, we delve into the power of personalized recommendations, examining how businesses leverage data-driven insights to deliver tailored experiences that delight customers and drive business growth.

1. Understanding Personalized Recommendations:

Personalized recommendations entail the use of data analytics and machine learning algorithms to deliver tailored suggestions to users based on their past behavior, preferences, and contextual information. By analyzing user interactions, purchase history, demographics, and browsing behavior, recommendation engines can identify patterns and trends to predict which products or content are most likely to resonate with each user. Personalized recommendations leverage various techniques, including collaborative filtering, content-based filtering, and hybrid approaches, to deliver relevant and timely suggestions that enhance the user experience and drive engagement.

2. Enhancing User Experience:

Personalized recommendations play a crucial role in enhancing the user experience by providing users with relevant and engaging content that aligns with their interests and preferences. By surfacing products, articles, or videos that are tailored to each user's tastes, recommendation engines help users discover new and interesting content that they may not have otherwise encountered. This not only increases user engagement and satisfaction but also encourages users to spend more time on the platform, driving ad revenue, and increasing customer lifetime value.

3. Driving Sales and Conversions:

Personalized recommendations have a significant impact on driving sales and conversions by guiding users towards products that match their preferences and purchase intent. By presenting users with relevant product recommendations at key touchpoints in the customer journey, such as product pages, checkout, or email campaigns, businesses can increase the likelihood of conversion and upsell complementary products. Moreover, personalized recommendations can help reduce decision fatigue and analysis paralysis by narrowing down the options and presenting users with curated selections that meet their needs and preferences.

4. Increasing Customer Engagement and Retention:

Personalized recommendations play a crucial role in increasing customer engagement and retention by fostering a deeper connection between users and the platform. By surfacing content that resonates with each user's interests and preferences, recommendation engines encourage users to return to the platform regularly, increasing user engagement and time spent on the site. Moreover, personalized recommendations can help strengthen brand loyalty by demonstrating an understanding of the user's needs and preferences, fostering a sense of trust and affinity towards the brand.

5. Optimizing Content Discovery:

Personalized recommendations optimize content discovery by helping users find relevant and interesting content amidst the vast sea of options available online. Whether it's discovering new music, movies, articles, or products, recommendation engines leverage data-driven insights to surface content that matches each user's tastes and preferences. This not only improves the user experience by reducing the effort required to find relevant content but also increases the likelihood of user engagement and interaction with the platform.

6. Challenges and Considerations:

While personalized recommendations offer numerous benefits, businesses must also navigate challenges and considerations to ensure the effectiveness and ethical use of recommendation algorithms. Challenges such as data privacy, algorithmic bias, and user trust require careful consideration and mitigation strategies to safeguard user rights and maintain trust. Moreover, businesses must continuously monitor and optimize recommendation algorithms to ensure relevance, accuracy, and fairness, as user preferences and behaviors evolve over time.

Customization and Privacy Concerns

In today's digital age, customization has become a cornerstone of the consumer experience, with businesses leveraging advanced technologies to tailor products, services, and recommendations to individual preferences and behaviors. While customization offers numerous benefits, including enhanced user engagement, satisfaction, and loyalty, it also raises significant privacy concerns related to data collection, usage, and protection. In this comprehensive exploration, we delve into the intersection of customization and privacy concerns, examining how businesses balance the desire for personalized experiences with the need to safeguard user privacy and data security.

1. The Rise of Customization:

Customization has become increasingly prevalent across various industries, driven by advancements in technology, data analytics, and consumer expectations. From personalized product recommendations and targeted advertising to customizable user interfaces and interactive experiences, customization enables businesses to deliver tailored experiences that meet the unique needs and preferences of individual users. By leveraging data-driven insights and machine learning algorithms, businesses can analyze user behavior, preferences, and demographics to personalize content, features, and offerings, enhancing the user experience and driving engagement.

2. Benefits of Customization:

Customization offers numerous benefits for both businesses and consumers. For businesses, customization can lead to increased sales, customer satisfaction, and brand loyalty by delivering personalized experiences that resonate with individual users. By tailoring products, services, and recommendations to specific user preferences and behaviors, businesses can differentiate themselves from competitors and create value-added experiences that drive customer retention and advocacy. For consumers, customization enhances the user experience by providing relevant content, recommendations, and features that align with their interests and preferences, reducing the time and effort required to find relevant information or products.

3. Privacy Concerns in Customization:

Despite the benefits of customization, it also raises significant privacy concerns related to data collection, usage, and protection. As businesses collect vast amounts of user data to power customization algorithms, there is a risk of unauthorized access, data breaches, and misuse of personal information. Moreover, the proliferation of third-party data brokers and ad networks further complicates the privacy landscape, as user data is often shared and monetized without explicit consent or awareness. Additionally, there are concerns about the transparency and accountability of customization algorithms, as users may not fully understand how their data is being used to personalize their experiences.

4. Data Collection Practices:

One of the primary privacy concerns in customization relates to data collection practices, as businesses collect and analyze vast amounts of user data to power personalized experiences. This data may include personal information such as name, email address, and location, as well as browsing history, purchase behavior, and social media activity. While businesses argue that this data is necessary to provide personalized experiences and improve service quality, critics raise concerns about the scope and granularity of data collection, as well as the lack of transparency and control over how user data is used and shared.

5. Data Usage and Sharing:

Another privacy concern in customization relates to the usage and sharing of user data with third parties, such as advertisers, data brokers, and business partners. As businesses monetize user data through targeted advertising and data licensing agreements, there is a risk that sensitive information may be shared or sold without user consent, leading to privacy violations and potential misuse of personal information. Moreover, the lack of transparency and oversight in data sharing practices makes it difficult for users to understand how their data is being used and who has access to it, raising concerns about data security and privacy.

6. Algorithmic Bias and Discrimination:

Algorithmic bias and discrimination are additional concerns in customization, as personalized algorithms may inadvertently perpetuate biases or stereotypes based on user demographics or behavior. For example, recommendation algorithms may inadvertently reinforce gender stereotypes by suggesting different products or content to male and female users, or they may inadvertently exclude certain demographic groups from opportunities or promotions. Moreover, the opacity of customization algorithms makes it difficult to detect and mitigate bias, leading to concerns about fairness, transparency, and accountability.

7. Regulatory and Ethical Considerations:

In response to growing privacy concerns, governments around the world have implemented regulations and guidelines to protect user data and ensure transparency and accountability in data practices. Regulations such as the General Data Protection Regulation (GDPR) in Europe and the California Consumer Privacy Act (CCPA) in the United States impose strict requirements on businesses regarding data collection, usage, and consent, as well as transparency and user rights. Moreover, businesses are increasingly adopting ethical frameworks and best practices to guide their customization efforts, such as principles of data minimization, user control, and algorithmic transparency.

8. Mitigating Privacy Concerns:

To mitigate privacy concerns in customization, businesses can adopt a variety of strategies and best practices to ensure transparency, accountability, and user control over their data. These include implementing robust data protection measures such as encryption, access controls, and data anonymization to safeguard user information from unauthorized access or misuse. Additionally, businesses can provide users with clear and concise privacy policies that explain how their data is collected, used, and shared, as well as their rights and options for controlling their privacy settings and preferences. Furthermore, businesses can leverage privacy-enhancing technologies such as differential privacy and federated learning to minimize the risk of privacy breaches while still delivering personalized experiences.

Chapter 9

Autonomous Systems From Self-Driving Cars to Robotics

Chapter 9 delves into the realm of autonomous systems, exploring the transformative impact of self-driving cars, robotics, and other intelligent machines on various industries and aspects of daily life. Autonomous systems represent a convergence of advanced technologies such as artificial intelligence, machine learning, and sensor technologies, enabling machines to perceive, navigate, and make decisions autonomously without human intervention. From revolutionizing transportation and logistics with self-driving vehicles to enhancing efficiency and productivity in manufacturing and healthcare with robotics, autonomous systems hold the promise of reshaping the way we live, work, and interact with the world around us.

In this chapter, we embark on a journey to uncover the underlying principles, applications, and implications of autonomous systems, examining the technical challenges, ethical considerations, and societal impacts of this rapidly advancing field. By exploring real-world examples and cutting-edge research, we aim to provide insights into the potential of autonomous systems to drive innovation, improve safety, and unlock new opportunities across a diverse range of industries and domains. Join us as we navigate the fascinating landscape of autonomous systems and envision the future of human-machine collaboration in an increasingly autonomous world.

Advancements in Autonomous Vehicles

Autonomous vehicles, once a futuristic concept, have rapidly transitioned from science fiction to reality, revolutionizing the transportation industry and reshaping the way we perceive mobility. These vehicles, equipped with sophisticated sensors, advanced algorithms, and artificial intelligence capabilities, can perceive their environment, make decisions, and navigate without human intervention. In this exploration of advancements in autonomous vehicles, we delve into the evolution of this transformative technology, examining the technical breakthroughs, challenges, and societal implications that have propelled its development.

1. Evolution of Autonomous Driving Technology:

The journey towards autonomous vehicles began with incremental advancements in vehicle automation, including features such as cruise control, automatic braking, and lane-keeping assistance. However, the emergence of artificial intelligence and machine learning has accelerated progress in autonomous driving technology, enabling vehicles to perceive and interpret their surroundings in real-time. From early experiments with adaptive cruise control and lane departure warnings to the development of fully autonomous prototypes, such as Google's Waymo and Tesla's Autopilot, the evolution of autonomous driving technology has been characterized by iterative improvements in sensor technology, computing power, and algorithmic sophistication.

2. Sensor Technologies:

Central to the operation of autonomous vehicles are sensor technologies that enable them to perceive and interpret their environment. These sensors include cameras, lidar (light detection and ranging), radar, and ultrasonic sensors, which provide complementary information about the vehicle's surroundings, including the detection of obstacles, pedestrians, and other vehicles. Recent advancements in sensor technology have focused on improving accuracy, range, and reliability, while reducing costs and size. For example, solid-state lidar and next-generation camera systems offer higher resolution and longer range capabilities, enhancing the perception capabilities of autonomous vehicles in diverse environmental conditions.

3. Artificial Intelligence and Machine Learning:

Artificial intelligence (AI) and machine learning (ML) play a crucial role in enabling autonomous vehicles to interpret sensor data, make decisions, and navigate complex environments. ML algorithms, trained on vast datasets of real-world driving scenarios, can learn to recognize patterns, predict behaviors, and adapt to dynamic situations. Deep learning techniques, such as convolutional neural networks (CNNs) and recurrent neural networks (RNNs), have shown remarkable success in perception tasks such as object detection, semantic segmentation, and scene understanding, enabling autonomous vehicles to accurately interpret their surroundings and react accordingly.

4. Mapping and Localization:

Accurate mapping and localization are essential for the safe and reliable operation of autonomous vehicles, allowing them to determine their position and navigate along predefined routes. High-definition maps, enriched with detailed information about road geometry, lane markings, and traffic signs, provide a reference for vehicle localization and route planning. Simultaneous localization and mapping (SLAM) algorithms enable vehicles to create and update maps in real-time using onboard sensors, such as lidar and cameras. Additionally, advancements in global navigation satellite systems (GNSS), such as GPS and Galileo, provide precise positioning information, further enhancing the accuracy of vehicle localization.

5. Safety and Reliability:

Ensuring the safety and reliability of autonomous vehicles is paramount to their widespread adoption and acceptance. Autonomous driving systems undergo rigorous testing and validation procedures, including simulations, closed-course testing, and real-world driving trials, to assess their performance and reliability in various scenarios. Safety-critical functions, such as perception, decision-making, and control, are redundantly designed and verified to mitigate the risk of system failures or malfunctions. Moreover, regulatory frameworks and industry standards, such as ISO 26262, provide guidelines for the development and certification of autonomous driving systems, ensuring compliance with safety requirements and best practices.

6. Challenges and Limitations:

Despite significant advancements, autonomous vehicles still face several technical, regulatory, and societal challenges that must be addressed to achieve widespread deployment and adoption. Technical challenges include the development of robust algorithms for complex driving scenarios, such as adverse weather conditions, construction zones, and unmapped environments. Regulatory challenges relate to the establishment of clear guidelines and standards for the testing, validation, and deployment of autonomous vehicles, ensuring their safety and compliance with existing traffic laws. Societal challenges encompass concerns about job displacement, ethical considerations, and the impact on urban planning and infrastructure

7. Future Outlook:

Looking ahead, the future of autonomous vehicles holds immense promise for transforming transportation, mobility, and urban living. Advancements in AI, sensor technology, and connectivity are expected to accelerate progress towards fully autonomous vehicles capable of navigating any environment and operating under diverse conditions. The integration of autonomous vehicles with smart city infrastructure, such as traffic management systems and vehicle-to-infrastructure (V2I) communication, promises to further improve safety, efficiency, and sustainability in urban mobility. Moreover, the advent of shared and on-demand autonomous mobility services has the potential to revolutionize the way people move and commute, reducing congestion, emissions, and the need for private car ownership.

Robotics Enhancing Automation Across Industries

Robotics has emerged as a transformative technology, revolutionizing automation across various industries and domains. From manufacturing and logistics to healthcare and agriculture, robots are increasingly being deployed to perform a wide range of tasks with precision, efficiency, and reliability. In this comprehensive exploration, we delve into the role of robotics in enhancing automation across industries, examining the advancements, applications, and implications of this rapidly evolving field.

1. Evolution of Robotics Technology:

Robotics technology has undergone significant evolution, driven by advancements in mechanical design, sensing capabilities, and artificial intelligence. Early industrial robots were primarily used for repetitive and hazardous tasks in manufacturing environments, such as assembly line operations and welding. However, recent advancements in robotics have led to the development of more versatile and intelligent robots capable of performing complex tasks in diverse environments. These advancements include the integration of sensors for perception and feedback, the use of advanced materials for lightweight and flexible design, and the adoption of AI and machine learning for adaptive and autonomous behavior.

2. Applications in Manufacturing and Automation:

Robotics plays a crucial role in manufacturing and automation, where robots are used to perform tasks such as assembly, welding, painting, and material handling. Industrial robots equipped with articulated arms and grippers can manipulate objects with precision and speed, increasing production efficiency and reducing labor costs. Collaborative robots, or cobots, work alongside human operators in shared workspaces, enhancing flexibility and safety in manufacturing environments. Moreover, robots are increasingly being used for tasks such as quality inspection, predictive maintenance, and inventory management, further optimizing production processes and improving product quality.

3. Logistics and Warehouse Automation:

Robotics is transforming logistics and warehouse operations, where robots are deployed to automate tasks such as picking, packing, and sorting of goods. Autonomous mobile robots (AMRs) navigate warehouse environments using sensors and onboard navigation systems, transporting goods between storage locations and fulfillment centers. Robotic arms and grippers are used for automated picking and sorting of items, reducing order fulfillment times and improving inventory accuracy. Additionally, drones and aerial robots are used for inventory management and surveillance in large warehouses and distribution centers, providing real-time visibility and monitoring of operations.

4. Healthcare and Medical Robotics:

Robotics is revolutionizing healthcare and medical practices, where robots are used for a wide range of applications, including surgery, rehabilitation, and patient care. Surgical robots, such as the da Vinci Surgical System, enable minimally invasive procedures with enhanced precision and dexterity, reducing patient recovery times and complications. Rehabilitation robots assist patients in regaining mobility and motor function following injury or surgery, providing personalized therapy and feedback. Service robots, such as telepresence robots and robotic assistants, support healthcare professionals in tasks such as patient monitoring, medication delivery, and disinfection of hospital environments

5. Agricultural Robotics and Precision Farming:

Robotics is reshaping agriculture and farming practices, where robots are used to automate tasks such as planting, harvesting, and crop monitoring. Autonomous tractors equipped with GPS and sensors can navigate fields and perform precision farming operations, such as planting seeds and applying fertilizers, with high accuracy and efficiency. Robotic harvesters use computer vision and machine learning algorithms to identify and pick ripe fruits and vegetables, reducing labor costs and increasing crop yields. Additionally, drones and aerial robots are used for aerial imaging and crop monitoring, providing farmers with valuable insights into crop health, moisture levels, and pest infestations.

6. Challenges and Considerations:

Despite the numerous benefits of robotics in enhancing automation across industries, there are several challenges and considerations that must be addressed to realize its full potential. Technical challenges include the development of robust and reliable robotic systems that can operate in diverse environments and conditions. Safety concerns arise from the interaction between robots and humans in shared workspaces, requiring the implementation of safety protocols and risk assessment procedures. Ethical considerations relate to the impact of automation on jobs, workers' rights, and societal inequalities, raising questions about the equitable distribution of benefits and risks associated with robotics

7. Future Outlook:

Looking ahead, the future of robotics holds immense promise for further enhancing automation across industries and domains. Advancements in AI, machine learning, and sensor technologies are expected to enable robots to perform increasingly complex tasks with greater autonomy and intelligence. Collaborative robots will continue to work alongside humans in shared workspaces, augmenting human capabilities and enhancing productivity. Moreover, robots will play a crucial role in addressing global challenges such as climate change, food security, and healthcare access, by enabling sustainable and efficient solutions through automation and innovation.

Chapter 10
AI and Creativity

Chapter 10 delves into the intriguing intersection of artificial intelligence (AI) and creativity, exploring how AI technologies are reshaping the landscape of artistic expression, design, and innovation. Traditionally, creativity has been regarded as a uniquely human trait, fueled by imagination, intuition, and emotional intelligence. However, recent advancements in AI have challenged this notion, with machines demonstrating the ability to generate original ideas, artworks, and designs autonomously.

In this chapter, we embark on a journey to uncover the role of AI in fostering creativity across various domains, from visual arts and music composition to literature and design. By examining the capabilities of AI algorithms such as generative adversarial networks (GANs), recurrent neural networks (RNNs), and deep learning models, we explore how machines are augmenting human creativity, expanding the boundaries of what is possible, and sparking new forms of artistic expression.

Through real-world examples, case studies, and expert insights, we aim to illuminate the potential of AI to inspire, collaborate with, and challenge human creators in the pursuit of innovation and self-expression. Join us as we unravel the fascinating interplay between AI and creativity, and envision the future of artistic collaboration and innovation in an AI-powered world.

AI in Art and Music

Art and music have long been regarded as quintessentially human expressions, driven by creativity, emotion, and cultural context. However, recent advancements in artificial intelligence (AI) have begun to challenge this perception, with machines demonstrating the ability to create original artworks and compose music autonomously. In this exploration of AI in art and music, we delve into the transformative impact of AI technologies on the creative process, examining how algorithms are reshaping the landscape of artistic expression, collaboration, and innovation.

1. Generative Adversarial Networks (GANs) in Art:

Generative Adversarial Networks (GANs) have emerged as a powerful tool for generating realistic and novel artworks. GANs consist of two neural networks - a generator and a discriminator - that are trained simultaneously to generate images that are indistinguishable from real ones. Artists and researchers have leveraged GANs to create a wide range of artworks, from paintings and drawings to digital sculptures and animations. By learning from large datasets of existing artworks, GANs can generate new images that mimic the style, composition, and subject matter of human-created art, blurring the lines between human and machine creativity.

2. AI-Generated Music Composition:

AI algorithms are also making waves in the field of music composition, where they are being used to create original compositions across various genres and styles. Recurrent Neural Networks (RNNs) and Long Short-Term Memory (LSTM) networks, in particular, have shown promise in generating melodies, harmonies, and entire musical compositions. By analyzing patterns and structures in existing music datasets, these algorithms can generate new music that exhibits characteristics similar to those of human-composed pieces. Moreover, AI-generated music can be tailored to specific preferences or constraints, such as mood, tempo, or instrumentation, making it a versatile tool for composers, producers, and artists.

3. Collaborative Creativity with AI:

AI is not only capable of generating art and music autonomously but also of collaborating with human creators to inspire and augment their creative process. Artists, musicians, and designers are increasingly incorporating AI tools and techniques into their workflows to explore new possibilities and push the boundaries of their creativity. For example, AI-powered tools such as style transfer algorithms and interactive generative models enable artists to experiment with different artistic styles and techniques, providing new avenues for exploration and expression. Similarly, musicians and composers are using AI-generated music as a source of inspiration or as a starting point for further refinement and development, fostering a symbiotic relationship between human and machine creativity.

4. Ethical and Aesthetic Considerations:

Despite the potential of AI in art and music, there are ethical and aesthetic considerations that must be addressed to ensure responsible and meaningful use of these technologies. One concern is the issue of authorship and ownership, as AI-generated artworks and music raise questions about the role of the creator and the value of originality in the creative process. Additionally, there are concerns about the homogenization of artistic expression and the potential loss of human creativity and diversity in an AI-dominated landscape. Moreover, there are ethical considerations surrounding the use of AI-generated content in commercial contexts, such as copyright infringement and fair compensation for artists and creators.

5. The Future of AI in Art and Music:

Looking ahead, the future of AI in art and music holds immense promise for unlocking new forms of creativity, collaboration, and expression. As AI algorithms continue to advance in sophistication and capabilities, they will enable artists, musicians, and designers to explore new creative territories and push the boundaries of what is possible. Moreover, AI-driven tools and platforms will democratize access to creative tools and resources, empowering individuals from diverse backgrounds to engage in artistic expression and innovation. However, it is essential to approach the integration of AI in art and music with caution and mindfulness, ensuring that these technologies are used responsibly and ethically to preserve the integrity and diversity of human creativity.

The Intersection of AI and Creativity

The intersection of artificial intelligence (AI) and creativity represents a fascinating and rapidly evolving frontier in the realm of technology and the arts. Traditionally, creativity has been viewed as a uniquely human trait, involving imagination, intuition, and emotional intelligence. However, recent advancements in AI have challenged this perception, with machines demonstrating the ability to generate original ideas, artworks, music, literature, and even inventions. In this exploration of the intersection of AI and creativity, we delve into the transformative impact of AI technologies on the creative process, examining how algorithms are reshaping the landscape of artistic expression, innovation, and collaboration.

1. Understanding AI Creativity:

AI creativity refers to the ability of artificial intelligence systems to generate novel and meaningful outputs across various domains, such as art, music, literature, and design. Unlike traditional AI applications that focus on problem-solving and optimization, AI creativity involves generating outputs that exhibit qualities typically associated with human creativity, such as originality, expressiveness, and emotional resonance. This can include generating artworks, composing music, writing poetry, designing products, and even inventing new concepts or ideas. AI creativity is made possible by leveraging techniques such as deep learning, generative modeling, reinforcement learning, and evolutionary algorithms, which enable machines to learn from data, explore possibilities, and generate new outputs autonomously.

2. Applications of AI Creativity:

AI creativity has diverse applications across various industries and domains, unlocking new possibilities for innovation, expression, and problem-solving. In the field of art and design, AI algorithms such as generative adversarial networks (GANs) and style transfer techniques enable machines to create original artworks, designs, and visualizations that push the boundaries of artistic expression and aesthetic exploration. Similarly, in music composition, AI algorithms such as recurrent neural networks (RNNs) and evolutionary algorithms can generate original compositions, melodies, and harmonies across different genres and styles, providing composers and musicians with new sources of inspiration and exploration. Moreover, AI creativity extends to fields such as literature, where algorithms can generate stories, poems, and essays, and to product design, where algorithms can generate innovative concepts and prototypes

3. Augmenting Human Creativity:

Rather than replacing human creativity, AI has the potential to augment and enhance human creativity by providing new tools, techniques, and sources of inspiration. Artists, designers, musicians, writers, and inventors are increasingly incorporating AI-driven tools and platforms into their creative workflows to explore new possibilities, experiment with different ideas, and overcome creative blocks. For example, artists can use AI-powered tools for image manipulation, style transfer, and content generation to explore new artistic styles and techniques. Similarly, musicians and composers can use AI-generated music as a source of inspiration or as a starting point for further exploration and refinement. By leveraging AI creativity, human creators can push the boundaries of their own creativity and explore new avenues of expression and innovation.

4. Ethical and Societal Implications:

Despite the potential of AI creativity, there are ethical and societal implications that must be considered to ensure responsible and meaningful use of these technologies. One concern is the issue of authorship and ownership, as AI-generated outputs raise questions about the role of the creator and the value of originality in the creative process. Additionally, there are concerns about the homogenization of creativity and the potential loss of human creativity and diversity in an AI-dominated landscape. Moreover, there are ethical considerations surrounding the use of AI-generated content in commercial contexts, such as copyright infringement and fair compensation for human creators. It is essential to address these ethical and societal concerns to ensure that AI creativity is used in ways that respect the rights and dignity of human creators and promote diversity and inclusivity in the creative process

5. The Future of AI Creativity:

Looking ahead, the future of AI creativity holds immense promise for unlocking new forms of expression, innovation, and collaboration. As AI algorithms continue to advance in sophistication and capabilities, they will enable human creators to explore new creative territories and push the boundaries of what is possible. Moreover, AI-driven tools and platforms will democratize access to creative tools and resources, empowering individuals from diverse backgrounds to engage in artistic expression and innovation. By embracing AI creativity and fostering collaboration between human and machine creators, we can harness the full potential of AI to inspire, augment, and enrich the creative landscape.

Chapter 11
Ethics and AI Navigating the Moral Landscape

Chapter 11 delves into the critical intersection of ethics and artificial intelligence (AI), navigating the complex moral landscape that arises from the increasing integration of AI technologies into various aspects of society. As AI systems become more pervasive and autonomous, they raise profound ethical questions about their impact on individuals, communities, and the world at large. In this exploration, we examine the ethical considerations surrounding the development, deployment, and governance of AI, seeking to understand how we can ensure that AI technologies are used in ways that promote fairness, transparency, accountability, and societal well-being.

AI systems have the potential to significantly impact various aspects of human life, from employment and healthcare to privacy and security. However, these advancements also come with ethical challenges, such as algorithmic bias, privacy violations, and automation-induced job displacement. By exploring these ethical dilemmas and engaging in critical reflection, we can work towards developing ethical frameworks, guidelines, and policies that guide the responsible development and use of AI. Through collaborative efforts involving policymakers, technologists, ethicists, and stakeholders, we can navigate the moral landscape of AI and shape a future where AI technologies serve the common good while upholding fundamental ethical principles and values.

Ethical Considerations in AI Development and Deployment

The rapid advancement of artificial intelligence (AI) technologies has brought about unprecedented opportunities and challenges, prompting a critical examination of the ethical implications associated with their development and deployment. As AI systems become increasingly integrated into various aspects of society, from healthcare and finance to transportation and education, it is imperative to consider the ethical considerations that arise from their use. In this exploration, we delve into the complex ethical landscape of AI, examining key considerations surrounding fairness, transparency, accountability, privacy, and societal impact.

1. Fairness and Bias:

One of the foremost ethical considerations in AI development is ensuring fairness and mitigating bias in algorithmic decision-making. AI systems trained on biased datasets or designed with biased algorithms can perpetuate and amplify existing societal inequalities, leading to discriminatory outcomes for certain individuals or groups. Addressing bias in AI requires careful consideration of dataset selection, algorithm design, and model evaluation to ensure that AI systems are equitable and inclusive. Techniques such as fairness-aware machine learning and bias mitigation strategies can help mitigate bias and promote fairness in AI systems, but ongoing vigilance and oversight are essential to address emerging biases and ensure equitable outcomes.

2. Transparency and Explainability:

Transparency and explainability are essential for fostering trust and accountability in AI systems, particularly in high-stakes domains such as healthcare, criminal justice, and finance. Users and stakeholders must be able to understand how AI systems make decisions, the factors that influence their outputs, and the potential implications of those decisions. Achieving transparency and explainability in AI requires clear documentation of algorithms and model architectures, as well as mechanisms for interpreting and visualizing model outputs. Moreover, techniques such as interpretable machine learning and explainable AI aim to provide insights into AI decision-making processes, enabling users to assess the reliability and validity of AI-generated recommendations or predictions.

3. Accountability and Responsibility:

Ensuring accountability and responsibility in AI development and deployment is essential for addressing the potential risks and harms associated with AI systems. Developers, manufacturers, and users of AI technologies must be held accountable for the ethical and societal implications of their products and decisions. This requires establishing clear lines of responsibility and liability for AI systems, as well as mechanisms for recourse and redress in the event of algorithmic errors, biases, or unintended consequences. Additionally, ethical guidelines and codes of conduct for AI practitioners can help promote responsible behavior and decision-making, emphasizing principles such as beneficence, non-maleficence, and respect for human dignity.

4. Privacy and Data Protection:

Privacy and data protection are fundamental rights that must be upheld in the development and deployment of AI systems. AI technologies often rely on large amounts of personal data to train and improve their performance, raising concerns about data privacy, consent, and surveillance. To protect privacy in AI, developers must implement robust data governance practices, such as data anonymization, encryption, and differential privacy, to safeguard sensitive information and prevent unauthorized access or misuse. Moreover, policymakers must enact legislation and regulations, such as the General Data Protection Regulation (GDPR) and the

California Consumer Privacy Act (CCPA), to ensure that individuals have control over their personal data and are informed about how it is used by AI systems.

5. Societal Impact and Inclusivity:

AI technologies have the potential to have profound societal impacts, influencing employment, education, healthcare, and social interactions. It is essential to consider the broader societal implications of AI deployment and ensure that these technologies promote social justice, equity, and inclusivity. This requires engaging diverse stakeholders, including marginalized communities, in the design, development, and deployment of AI systems to ensure that they reflect the needs and values of society as a whole. Moreover, efforts to address the digital divide and promote digital literacy can help mitigate the risk of exacerbating existing inequalities and ensure that the benefits of AI are accessible to all members of society.

Ensuring Transparency and Accountability in AI Development and Deployment

Transparency and accountability are essential pillars of responsible AI development and deployment, ensuring that AI systems are trustworthy, fair, and aligned with societal values. As AI technologies become increasingly integrated into various aspects of society, from healthcare and finance to criminal justice and education, there is a growing need to ensure that these systems are transparent in their decision-making processes and accountable for their actions. In this exploration, we delve into the importance of transparency and accountability in AI, examining key considerations, challenges, and strategies for ensuring transparency and accountability throughout the AI lifecycle.

1. The Importance of Transparency and Accountability:

Transparency refers to the openness and clarity of AI systems, enabling users and stakeholders to understand how AI systems work, the factors that influence their decisions, and the potential implications of those decisions. Accountability, on the other hand, refers to the responsibility and liability of developers, manufacturers, and users of AI systems for the ethical and societal implications of their products and decisions. Transparency and accountability are essential for fostering trust, fairness, and accountability in AI, promoting confidence among users, stakeholders, and the public in the reliability and integrity of AI systems.

2. Challenges in Achieving Transparency and Accountability:

Achieving transparency and accountability in AI development and deployment poses several challenges, stemming from the complexity, opacity, and autonomy of AI systems. AI algorithms, particularly deep learning models, are often complex and opaque, making it difficult to interpret and understand their decision-making processes. Moreover, AI systems can exhibit biases, errors, and unintended consequences, leading to ethical and societal implications that are difficult to anticipate or mitigate. Additionally, the lack of standardization and regulation in the AI industry can hinder efforts to ensure transparency and accountability, as developers may prioritize commercial interests over ethical considerations.

3. Strategies for Ensuring Transparency and Accountability:

Despite the challenges, there are several strategies and best practices that can be adopted to ensure transparency and accountability in AI development and deployment:

a) **Documentation and Explanation:** Developers should document their AI systems, including algorithms, data sources, and decision-making processes, in a clear and accessible manner. This documentation should provide insights into how AI systems work, the factors that influence their decisions, and the potential implications of those decisions.

b) **Model Interpretability:** Techniques such as interpretable machine learning and explainable AI aim to provide insights into AI decision-making processes, enabling users to understand and interpret the outputs of AI systems. This can help build trust and confidence in AI systems by providing transparency into their inner workings.

c) **Algorithmic Auditing:** Independent audits and evaluations of AI systems can help identify biases, errors, and unintended consequences, ensuring that AI systems are fair, reliable, and aligned with ethical principles. Algorithmic auditing involves examining the inputs, outputs, and behavior of AI systems to assess their performance and identify areas for improvement.

d) **Ethical Guidelines and Standards:** The development and adoption of ethical guidelines, standards, and best practices for AI can help promote transparency and accountability in AI development and deployment. Organizations such as the IEEE, ACM, and Partnership on AI have developed frameworks and principles for ethical AI that emphasize transparency, fairness, and accountability.

e) **Regulatory Oversight:** Policymakers and regulators play a crucial role in ensuring transparency and accountability in AI development and deployment. By enacting legislation and regulations, such as the General Data Protection Regulation (GDPR) and the Algorithmic Accountability Act, policymakers can establish clear guidelines and requirements for the responsible use of AI and hold developers and users accountable for the ethical and societal implications of AI systems.

4. Case Studies and Examples:

Examining real-world case studies and examples of transparency and accountability in AI can provide insights into best practices and lessons learned. For example, the development of AI explainability tools such as LIME (Local Interpretable Model-agnostic Explanations) and SHAP (SHapley Additive exPlanations) has enabled researchers and practitioners to interpret and explain the predictions of complex AI models, promoting transparency and trust in AI systems. Similarly, initiatives such as the AI Incident Database and the AI Ethics Impact Group provide platforms for sharing knowledge, experiences, and lessons learned from incidents involving AI systems, helping to inform best practices and guidelines for ensuring transparency and accountability in AI.

5. Future Directions and Considerations:

Ensuring transparency and accountability in AI development and deployment is an ongoing and evolving challenge that requires collaborative efforts from developers, policymakers, researchers, and stakeholders. Moving forward, it is essential to continue advancing techniques and strategies for achieving transparency and accountability in AI, while also addressing emerging challenges and considerations such as the ethical use of AI in sensitive domains, the role of AI in exacerbating societal inequalities, and the need for international cooperation and coordination in AI governance.

Chapter 12
The Future of AI Opportunities and Challenges

Chapter 12 explores the dynamic landscape of the future of artificial intelligence (AI), presenting a nuanced examination of the opportunities and challenges that lie ahead as AI continues to evolve and proliferate across various domains. As AI technologies become increasingly integrated into society, from healthcare and transportation to finance and education, it is essential to anticipate the potential impacts and implications of these advancements. In this exploration, we delve into the transformative potential of AI to drive innovation, enhance productivity, and address complex societal challenges, while also considering the ethical, social, and economic considerations that must be addressed to ensure responsible and equitable deployment of AI technologies. By examining emerging trends, breakthroughs, and dilemmas in the field of AI, we aim to provide insights into the opportunities and challenges that will shape the future of AI and inform strategies for navigating this rapidly evolving landscape in a manner that promotes human well-being, prosperity, and progress.

Emerging Trends in AI Research and Development

Artificial intelligence (AI) continues to evolve at a rapid pace, with ongoing research and development efforts pushing the boundaries of what is possible in terms of AI capabilities and applications. In this exploration, we delve into the emerging trends shaping the landscape of AI research and development, from breakthroughs in machine learning and neural networks to innovations in natural language processing, robotics, and beyond. By examining these trends, we gain insights into the cutting-edge technologies, methodologies, and applications that are driving the future of AI and shaping the way we interact with technology.

1. Advancements in Deep Learning:

Deep learning, a subset of machine learning, has been at the forefront of AI research and development in recent years, driving breakthroughs in areas such as computer vision, natural language processing, and speech recognition. Advancements in deep learning architectures, such as convolutional neural networks (CNNs) and recurrent neural networks (RNNs), have enabled significant improvements in AI performance and capabilities. Additionally, techniques such as transfer learning, self-supervised learning, and reinforcement learning have expanded the applicability of deep learning models to a wide range of tasks and domains, from image classification and object detection to language translation and dialogue generation.

2. Continued Progress in Natural Language Processing (NLP):

Natural language processing (NLP) has seen remarkable progress in recent years, driven by advancements in deep learning models and techniques. Transformer-based architectures, such as the BERT (Bidirectional Encoder Representations from Transformers) model, have revolutionized the field of NLP by enabling pre-training on large text corpora and fine-tuning for specific downstream tasks. These models have achieved state-of-the-art performance on a wide range of NLP tasks, including language understanding, sentiment analysis, question answering, and language generation. Moreover, research efforts in areas such as multilingual NLP, zero-shot learning, and commonsense reasoning are pushing the boundaries of what is possible in NLP and paving the way for more sophisticated AI systems that can understand and generate human-like text.

3. Exponential Growth in Data and Computing Resources:

The exponential growth in data availability and computing resources has fueled advancements in AI research and development, enabling the training of larger and more complex models with unprecedented scale and efficiency. The proliferation of big data sources, such as social media, sensor networks, and IoT devices, has provided researchers with vast amounts of data for training and testing AI models. Additionally, the availability of high-performance computing resources, such as GPUs (Graphics Processing Units) and TPUs (Tensor Processing Units), has accelerated the training and inference of deep learning models, reducing the time and cost required to develop and deploy AI systems.

4. Interdisciplinary Collaboration and Cross-Domain Applications:

Interdisciplinary collaboration and cross-domain applications have become increasingly prevalent in AI research and development, as researchers seek to leverage insights and techniques from diverse fields to tackle complex real-world problems. For example, AI techniques developed in the field of computer vision are being applied to medical imaging for disease diagnosis and treatment planning. Similarly, AI techniques developed in natural language processing are being applied to legal research, customer service, and content creation. These interdisciplinary collaborations are driving innovation and pushing the boundaries of AI applications in domains ranging from healthcare and finance to agriculture and entertainment.

5. Ethical and Societal Considerations:

With the increasing integration of AI technologies into society, there is growing awareness of the ethical and societal implications associated with AI research and development. Concerns about algorithmic bias, privacy violations, job displacement, and autonomous weapons have prompted calls for responsible and ethical AI development practices. Researchers, policymakers, and industry stakeholders are grappling with these challenges and working to develop frameworks, guidelines, and regulations to ensure that AI technologies are developed and deployed in ways that promote fairness, transparency, accountability, and societal well-being.

6. Exploration of New Frontiers: Quantum Computing, Edge AI, and Beyond:

Beyond the current state-of-the-art in AI, researchers are exploring new frontiers and emerging technologies that have the potential to revolutionize the field. Quantum computing, for example, holds promise for solving complex optimization problems and accelerating AI algorithms such as matrix factorization and quantum machine learning. Edge AI, on the other hand, involves deploying AI models directly on edge devices such as smartphones, wearables, and IoT devices, enabling real-time inference and decision-making without relying on cloud-based servers. These emerging technologies represent exciting opportunities for further advancing the capabilities and applications of AI in the future.

Addressing Challenges and Shaping the Future of AI

As artificial intelligence (AI) continues to advance and permeate various aspects of society, it is crucial to address the challenges and opportunities that lie ahead to shape the future of AI in a responsible and beneficial manner. In this exploration, we delve into the key challenges facing AI development and deployment and discuss strategies for addressing these challenges to ensure that AI technologies contribute positively to society.

1. Ethical and Societal Implications:

One of the primary challenges facing AI is the ethical and societal implications associated with its development and deployment. Concerns such as algorithmic bias, privacy violations, job displacement, and autonomous weapons have prompted calls for responsible and ethical AI practices. To address these concerns, researchers, policymakers, and industry stakeholders must work together to develop frameworks, guidelines, and regulations that promote fairness, transparency, accountability, and societal well-being in AI development and deployment.

2. Algorithmic Bias and Fairness:

Algorithmic bias poses a significant challenge in AI development, as AI systems trained on biased datasets can perpetuate and amplify existing societal inequalities. To address algorithmic bias, researchers must develop techniques for detecting and mitigating bias in AI algorithms and datasets. Additionally, efforts to promote diversity and inclusivity in AI research and development can help mitigate bias and ensure that AI technologies are fair and equitable for all users.

3. Privacy and Data Protection:

Privacy and data protection are critical considerations in AI development, as AI systems often rely on large amounts of personal data to train and improve their performance. To protect privacy in AI, developers must implement robust data governance practices, such as data anonymization, encryption, and differential privacy, to safeguard sensitive information and prevent unauthorized access or misuse. Moreover, policymakers must enact legislation and regulations to ensure that individuals have control over their personal data and are informed about how it is used by AI systems.

4. Transparency and Accountability:

Transparency and accountability are essential for fostering trust and confidence in AI systems. Developers must provide clear documentation of AI systems, including algorithms, data sources, and decision-making processes, to enable users and stakeholders to understand how AI systems work and the factors that influence their decisions. Additionally, mechanisms for interpreting and visualizing model outputs can help promote transparency and accountability in AI decision-making.

5. Cybersecurity and Robustness:

Cybersecurity and robustness are critical considerations in AI development, as AI systems are vulnerable to attacks and adversarial manipulation. Developers must implement robust security measures to protect AI systems from cyber threats and ensure that they are resilient to adversarial attacks. Techniques such as adversarial training and model hardening can help improve the robustness and security of AI systems, reducing the risk of exploitation and misuse.

6. Education and Workforce Development:

Education and workforce development are essential for preparing individuals for the future of work in an AI-driven world. As AI technologies continue to evolve and automate various tasks and industries, there is a growing need for skilled professionals who can develop, deploy, and maintain AI systems. To address this need, educational institutions must incorporate AI education and training into their curricula, providing students with the knowledge and skills they need to succeed in an AI-powered workforce.

7. International Cooperation and Governance:

International cooperation and governance are essential for addressing the global challenges posed by AI and ensuring that AI technologies are developed and deployed in ways that promote peace, security, and prosperity. Multilateral organizations, such as the United Nations and the OECD, play a crucial role in facilitating dialogue and cooperation among countries and promoting responsible AI governance. Additionally, efforts to develop international standards and norms for AI development and deployment can help foster trust and collaboration among countries and promote the responsible use of AI technologies on a global scale.

Chapter 13

Ethical Frameworks and Guidelines

Chapter 13 delves into the critical importance of ethical frameworks and guidelines in the development and deployment of artificial intelligence (AI) technologies. As AI continues to advance and become increasingly integrated into various aspects of society, it is essential to establish clear ethical principles and guidelines to ensure that AI systems are developed and used in ways that are fair, transparent, and accountable. This chapter explores the foundational principles of ethical AI, including fairness, transparency, accountability, and societal impact, and examines the challenges and opportunities associated with implementing these principles in practice.

Ethical frameworks provide a roadmap for AI developers, policymakers, and stakeholders to navigate the complex ethical considerations inherent in AI technologies. By adhering to ethical guidelines, developers can mitigate the risks of algorithmic bias, privacy violations, and unintended consequences, while promoting the responsible and ethical use of AI. Moreover, ethical frameworks serve as a foundation for building trust and confidence among users, stakeholders, and the public, fostering a culture of transparency and accountability in AI development and deployment.

Through the exploration of ethical frameworks and guidelines, this chapter aims to provide insights into the principles and practices that underpin ethical AI, and to equip readers with the knowledge and tools they need to navigate the ethical complexities of AI in a rapidly evolving technological landscape. By embracing ethical AI principles and guidelines, we can harness the transformative potential of AI technologies to benefit society while upholding fundamental ethical values and principles.

Introduction to Ethical Frameworks in AI Development

Artificial intelligence (AI) holds immense promise to transform industries, revolutionize processes, and enhance human lives. However, the rapid advancement of AI technologies has also raised significant ethical concerns regarding their development and deployment. From issues of fairness and accountability to questions about privacy and bias, the ethical dimensions of AI are complex and multifaceted. In response to these challenges, ethical frameworks have emerged as essential tools for guiding AI development in a responsible and socially beneficial manner.

1. Understanding Ethical Frameworks:

Ethical frameworks in AI development serve as guiding principles and guidelines to ensure that AI technologies are developed and deployed in ways that align with fundamental ethical values and principles. These frameworks provide a roadmap for AI developers, researchers, policymakers, and stakeholders to navigate the complex ethical considerations inherent in AI technologies. By adhering to ethical frameworks, stakeholders can mitigate the risks of harmful outcomes, such as algorithmic bias, privacy violations, and discrimination, while promoting the responsible and ethical use of AI.

Ethical frameworks typically encompass a set of principles and guidelines that address key ethical concerns, such as fairness, transparency, accountability, privacy, and societal impact. These principles are designed to uphold fundamental ethical values, such as respect for human dignity, fairness, justice, and the common good. Ethical frameworks may also include mechanisms for assessing and mitigating ethical risks, as well as guidelines for ethical decision-making and governance processes.

2. Key Principles of Ethical Frameworks:

Ethical frameworks in AI development are founded on a set of key principles that guide ethical decision-making and practice. These principles are derived from ethical theories and philosophies, as well as legal and regulatory standards, and are intended to promote the ethical and responsible development and deployment of AI technologies. Some of the key principles of ethical frameworks in AI development include:

- **Fairness and Equity:** Ensuring that AI systems are fair and equitable, and do not discriminate against individuals or groups based on factors such as race, gender, or socioeconomic status.

- **Transparency and Accountability:** Promoting transparency in AI systems, including openness about how AI systems work, the factors that influence their decisions, and the potential implications of those decisions. Additionally, ensuring accountability for the actions and decisions of AI systems, including mechanisms for redress and recourse in the event of harm or wrongdoing.

- **Privacy and Data Protection:** Protecting the privacy and data rights of individuals, including ensuring that AI systems adhere to privacy principles such as data minimization, purpose limitation, and user consent. Additionally, implementing robust data governance practices to safeguard sensitive information and prevent unauthorized access or misuse.

- **Societal Impact and Responsibility:** Considering the broader societal implications of AI technologies, including their impact on employment, education, healthcare, and social equity. Additionally, promoting social responsibility and ethical leadership in AI development and deployment, including engaging with diverse stakeholders and communities to understand their needs and concerns.

- **Human-Centered Design:** Designing AI systems with a focus on human values, needs, and experiences, and ensuring that AI technologies are developed and deployed in ways that enhance human well-being and autonomy. Additionally, promoting human agency and decision-making in the design and use of AI systems, and avoiding the use of AI technologies to manipulate or control human behavior.

3. Challenges and Considerations:

While ethical frameworks provide valuable guidance for AI development, they also present challenges and considerations that must be addressed to ensure their effectiveness and relevance in practice. Some of the key challenges and considerations include:

- **Cultural and Contextual Differences:** Ethical frameworks must be sensitive to cultural and contextual differences, as ethical values and norms may vary across different cultures and societies. Additionally, ethical frameworks must be adaptable and flexible to accommodate evolving ethical standards and practices.

- **Implementation and Enforcement:** Ethical frameworks are only effective if they are implemented and enforced effectively. This requires buy-in and commitment from stakeholders across all levels of the AI ecosystem, as well as mechanisms for monitoring, evaluating, and enforcing compliance with ethical principles and guidelines.

- **Trade-Offs and Conflicts:** Ethical decision-making in AI development often involves trade-offs and conflicts between competing ethical principles and values. For example, there may be tensions between maximizing accuracy and fairness in AI algorithms, or between protecting privacy and promoting innovation. Ethical frameworks must provide guidance for navigating these trade-offs and conflicts in a principled and transparent manner.

- **Interdisciplinary Collaboration:** Ethical frameworks in AI development require interdisciplinary collaboration and engagement, bringing together experts from diverse fields such as ethics, law, sociology, psychology, and computer science. This collaboration is essential for developing comprehensive and robust ethical frameworks that address the multifaceted ethical considerations inherent in AI technologies.

4. Examples of Ethical Frameworks:

Numerous organizations and initiatives have developed ethical frameworks and guidelines for AI development and deployment. Some of the notable examples include:

The IEEE Global Initiative on Ethics of Autonomous and Intelligent Systems: The IEEE has developed a series of standards and guidelines for ethical AI, including the Ethically Aligned Design framework, which provides principles and recommendations for designing ethically aligned AI systems.

- **The European Union's Ethics Guidelines for Trustworthy AI:** The European Union has developed a set of ethics guidelines for trustworthy AI, which include principles such as human agency and oversight, technical robustness and safety, privacy and data governance, transparency, and accountability.

- **The Principles for AI developed by the Future of Life Institute:** The Future of Life Institute has developed a set of principles for AI, which include goals such as avoiding the creation of AI systems that can harm humanity, ensuring that AI systems are robust and safe, and promoting transparency and accountability in AI development and deployment.

Principles of Ethical AI: Fairness, Transparency, Accountability

In the realm of artificial intelligence (AI), ensuring that systems are developed and deployed ethically is paramount. Ethical AI encompasses a set of principles that guide the design, development, and deployment of AI systems to ensure they are fair, transparent, and accountable. Among these principles, fairness, transparency, and accountability stand out as foundational pillars, guiding the ethical development and deployment of AI technologies. In this exploration, we delve into these principles, examining their significance, challenges, and implications in the context of AI development and deployment.

1. Fairness in AI:

Fairness in AI refers to the principle of ensuring that AI systems treat all individuals and groups fairly and without bias. In an ideal world, AI systems should make decisions based solely on relevant factors, such as merit or qualifications, without discriminating against individuals based on irrelevant factors, such as race, gender, or socioeconomic status. Achieving fairness in AI is challenging due to the complexity of human biases, the limitations of data, and the inherent trade-offs between different notions of fairness.

- One approach to promoting fairness in AI is through algorithmic fairness, which involves designing AI algorithms that mitigate biases and ensure equitable outcomes for all individuals and groups. Techniques such as fairness-aware machine learning, bias mitigation, and fairness constraints can help address biases in AI algorithms and promote fairness in decision-making processes. However, achieving fairness in AI requires careful consideration of the context, stakeholders, and potential trade-offs involved, as well as ongoing monitoring and evaluation to assess the impact of AI systems on different groups and communities.

2. Transparency in AI:

Transparency in AI refers to the principle of openness and clarity in AI systems, enabling users and stakeholders to understand how AI systems work, the factors that influence their decisions, and the potential implications of those decisions. Transparency is essential for promoting trust, accountability, and informed decision-making in AI development and deployment. Without transparency, users may not understand how AI systems work or how they make decisions, leading to mistrust, uncertainty, and potential misuse of AI technologies.

- There are several dimensions of transparency in AI, including algorithmic transparency, process transparency, and outcome transparency. Algorithmic transparency involves making AI algorithms and decision-making processes understandable and interpretable to users and stakeholders, enabling them to understand how AI systems work and why they make certain decisions. Process transparency involves providing insights into the development and deployment processes of AI systems, including data sources, model training, and evaluation methodologies. Outcome transparency involves making the outcomes and impacts of AI systems transparent and accountable, enabling users to assess the fairness, accuracy, and reliability of AI systems in practice.

3. Accountability in AI:

Accountability in AI refers to the principle of holding AI developers, manufacturers, and users responsible for the ethical and societal implications of AI technologies. Accountability is essential for ensuring that AI systems are developed and used in ways that promote fairness, transparency, and societal well-being, while also providing mechanisms for redress and recourse in the event of harm or wrongdoing. Without accountability, there is a risk that AI systems may be developed and deployed without adequate consideration of their ethical implications, leading to unintended consequences and potential harm to individuals and communities.

- There are several dimensions of accountability in AI, including legal accountability, organizational accountability, and social accountability. Legal accountability involves ensuring that AI developers, manufacturers, and users comply with relevant laws, regulations, and standards governing AI development and deployment, and are held liable for any harm caused by AI technologies. Organizational accountability involves establishing clear roles, responsibilities, and processes within organizations for ensuring the ethical and responsible development and deployment of AI technologies. Social accountability involves engaging with diverse stakeholders and communities to understand their needs, concerns, and perspectives on AI technologies, and incorporating their feedback into the development and deployment processes.

- Achieving accountability in AI requires collaboration and cooperation among AI developers, policymakers, industry stakeholders, and civil society organizations to develop and implement mechanisms for ensuring that AI technologies are developed and used in ways that promote ethical and societal values. This may include establishing codes of conduct, certification programs, and oversight mechanisms for AI development and deployment, as well as promoting transparency and accountability in AI decision-making processes.

Case Studies Ethical Dilemmas and Solutions in AI Deployment

Real-world deployment of artificial intelligence (AI) technologies often presents complex ethical dilemmas that require careful consideration and innovative solutions. From issues of algorithmic bias and discrimination to concerns about privacy violations and unintended consequences, ethical dilemmas in AI deployment are diverse and multifaceted. In this exploration, we examine several case studies that highlight ethical dilemmas faced in the deployment of AI technologies across various domains, and discuss potential solutions and strategies for addressing these challenges.

1. Algorithmic Bias in Criminal Justice:

Case Study: In the criminal justice system, AI algorithms are increasingly being used to assess risk, predict recidivism, and inform decisions about bail, sentencing, and parole. However, studies have shown that these algorithms can be biased against certain demographic groups, leading to unfair and discriminatory outcomes. For example, a study by ProPublica found that a widely used risk assessment tool in the United

States was biased against African American defendants, leading to higher rates of false positives for this group.

Solution: To address algorithmic bias in criminal justice AI systems, several approaches can be considered. One approach is to improve the fairness and transparency of AI algorithms by using techniques such as fairness-aware machine learning, bias mitigation, and fairness constraints. Additionally, policymakers and stakeholders can implement oversight mechanisms and accountability measures to monitor and evaluate the performance of AI algorithms in practice, and to ensure that they adhere to ethical and legal standards.

2. Privacy Concerns in Healthcare:

Case Study: In the healthcare sector, AI technologies are being used to analyze patient data, diagnose diseases, and personalize treatment plans. However, the use of AI in healthcare raises significant privacy concerns, as patient data is often sensitive and highly personal. There is a risk that AI algorithms could be used to identify individuals or disclose sensitive medical information without their consent, leading to breaches of privacy and confidentiality.

Solution: To address privacy concerns in healthcare AI, organizations can implement robust data governance practices, such as data anonymization, encryption, and differential privacy, to safeguard patient data and prevent unauthorized access or misuse. Additionally, policymakers can enact legislation and regulations, such as the Health Insurance Portability and Accountability Act (HIPAA) in the United States, to protect patient privacy and ensure that AI technologies comply with ethical and legal standards for data privacy and security.

3. Ethical Considerations in Autonomous Vehicles:

Case Study: Autonomous vehicles (AVs) hold the promise of reducing traffic accidents, improving road safety, and enhancing mobility for individuals with disabilities. However, the deployment of AVs also raises ethical considerations regarding safety, liability, and decision-making in the event of accidents. For example, AVs must make split-second decisions about how to respond to potentially life-threatening situations, such as avoiding a collision with a pedestrian or another vehicle.

Solution: To address ethical considerations in AV deployment, stakeholders can adopt a multidisciplinary approach that considers technical, legal, and ethical perspectives. This may involve developing ethical guidelines and decision-making frameworks for AVs that prioritize human safety and well-being, while also promoting transparency and accountability in AV development and deployment. Additionally, policymakers can establish regulatory frameworks and liability standards for AVs that hold manufacturers accountable for the safety and ethical behavior of their vehicles.

4. Bias in Hiring and Recruitment:

Case Study: AI algorithms are increasingly being used in hiring and recruitment processes to screen job applicants, assess qualifications, and make hiring decisions. However, studies have shown that these algorithms can be biased against certain demographic groups, leading to discrimination and unfair outcomes. For example, a study by researchers at MIT found that an AI recruiting tool developed by Amazon was biased against women, resulting in the system downgrading resumes that included the word "women's" or contained other indicators of gender.

Solution: To address bias in hiring and recruitment AI, organizations can implement fairness-aware machine learning techniques and bias mitigation strategies to ensure that AI algorithms do not discriminate against individuals based on protected characteristics such as race, gender, or age. Additionally, organizations can adopt transparency and accountability measures to monitor and evaluate the performance of AI algorithms in hiring and recruitment processes, and to ensure that they comply with ethical and legal standards for equal opportunity and nondiscrimination.

Implementing Ethical Guidelines: Challenges and Best Practices

Ethical guidelines play a crucial role in guiding the development and deployment of artificial intelligence (AI) technologies in a responsible and ethical manner. These guidelines provide a framework for AI developers, researchers, policymakers, and stakeholders to navigate the complex ethical considerations inherent in AI technologies and ensure that they are developed and used in ways that promote fairness, transparency, and accountability. However, implementing ethical guidelines presents its own set of challenges and complexities, requiring careful consideration and innovative solutions. In this exploration, we examine the challenges and best practices associated with implementing ethical guidelines in AI development and deployment.

1. Challenges in Implementing Ethical Guidelines:

Implementing ethical guidelines in AI development and deployment presents several challenges that must be addressed to ensure their effectiveness and relevance in practice. Some of the key challenges include:

- **Complexity and Interdisciplinarity:** AI development is a multidisciplinary endeavor that involves expertise from diverse fields such as computer science, ethics, law, sociology, psychology, and public policy. Implementing ethical guidelines requires collaboration and cooperation among stakeholders from these diverse disciplines, which can be challenging due to differences in terminology, methodologies, and priorities.

- **Lack of Consensus and Standardization:** Ethical guidelines in AI are often subject to interpretation and debate, leading to a lack of consensus and standardization across different frameworks and initiatives. This lack of consensus can create confusion and uncertainty among AI developers, policymakers, and stakeholders, making it difficult to establish clear and consistent ethical standards and practices.

- **Technological Complexity and Uncertainty:** AI technologies are rapidly evolving and becoming increasingly complex, making it difficult to anticipate and address the ethical implications of emerging technologies. Additionally, AI systems are often opaque and unpredictable, making it challenging to understand how they work and how they make decisions. This technological complexity and uncertainty can pose challenges for implementing ethical guidelines and ensuring that AI technologies are developed and used in ways that align with ethical values and principles.

- **Resource Constraints and Trade-Offs:** Implementing ethical guidelines in AI development and deployment requires significant resources, including time, expertise, and financial investment. However, organizations may face resource constraints and trade-offs that limit their ability to fully implement ethical guidelines. For example, organizations may prioritize speed and efficiency over ethical considerations in order to meet tight deadlines or compete in the market, leading to compromises in ethical practice.

2. Best Practices for Implementing Ethical Guidelines:

Despite the challenges, there are several best practices that organizations can adopt to effectively implement ethical guidelines in AI development and deployment. Some of the key best practices include:

- **Stakeholder Engagement and Collaboration:** Engage with diverse stakeholders, including AI developers, researchers, policymakers, industry stakeholders, civil society organizations, and affected communities, to understand their perspectives, needs, and concerns regarding ethical guidelines. Foster collaboration and cooperation among stakeholders to develop consensus on ethical standards and practices, and to ensure that ethical guidelines are relevant and meaningful to all stakeholders.

- **Ethical Impact Assessment:** Conduct ethical impact assessments to identify and assess the potential ethical implications of AI technologies throughout the development and deployment lifecycle. This may include assessing risks related to fairness, transparency, accountability, privacy, bias, discrimination, and unintended consequences. Use the findings of ethical impact assessments to inform decision-making and prioritize ethical considerations in AI development and deployment.

- **Ethical Design and Development:** Integrate ethical considerations into the design and development of AI technologies from the outset. Adopt design principles such as human-centered design, fairness by design, and privacy by design to ensure that AI technologies are developed in ways that prioritize human well-being, fairness, transparency, and accountability. Incorporate mechanisms for detecting and mitigating bias, discrimination, and other ethical risks throughout the development process.

- **Transparency and Accountability Mechanisms:** Implement transparency and accountability mechanisms to promote openness, trust, and accountability in AI development and deployment. This may include providing clear documentation of AI systems, including algorithms, data sources, and decision-making processes, to enable users and stakeholders to understand how AI systems work and the factors that influence their decisions. Additionally, establish mechanisms for interpreting and visualizing model outputs, as well as mechanisms for redress and recourse in the event of harm or wrongdoing.

- **Continuous Monitoring and Evaluation:** Continuously monitor and evaluate the performance of AI technologies in practice to assess their impact on ethical values and principles. Use feedback from users, stakeholders, and affected communities to identify areas for improvement and to refine ethical guidelines and practices over time. Adopt a culture of learning and adaptation that promotes continuous improvement in ethical practice and ensures that AI technologies are developed and used in ways that promote human well-being and societal welfare.

The Role of Stakeholders: Collaborating for Ethical AI Development

Ethical AI development requires collaboration and cooperation among diverse stakeholders, including AI developers, researchers, policymakers, industry stakeholders, civil society organizations, and affected communities. Each stakeholder plays a unique role in shaping the ethical development and deployment of AI technologies, and their collaboration is essential for ensuring that AI technologies are developed and used in ways that promote fairness, transparency, and accountability. In this exploration, we examine the role of stakeholders in ethical AI development and discuss strategies for fostering collaboration and cooperation among stakeholders.

1. Stakeholder Perspectives on Ethical AI:

- **AI Developers and Researchers:** AI developers and researchers are responsible for designing, developing, and testing AI technologies. They play a critical role in integrating ethical considerations into the design and development process, ensuring that AI technologies are developed in ways that prioritize human well-being, fairness, transparency, and accountability. AI developers and researchers are also responsible for identifying and addressing potential ethical risks and challenges associated with AI technologies, such as bias, discrimination, privacy violations, and unintended consequences.

- **Policymakers and Regulators:** Policymakers and regulators are responsible for creating and enforcing laws, regulations, and standards governing AI development and deployment. They play a crucial role in establishing the legal and regulatory frameworks that govern AI technologies, ensuring that they adhere to ethical and legal standards for fairness, transparency, accountability, privacy, and human rights. Policymakers and regulators also have a responsibility to engage with stakeholders and communities to understand their perspectives, needs, and concerns regarding AI technologies, and to incorporate these insights into the development of ethical guidelines and regulations.

- **Industry Stakeholders:** Industry stakeholders, including technology companies, startups, and corporations, play a significant role in driving AI innovation and adoption. They have a responsibility to develop and deploy AI technologies in ways that promote ethical values and principles, such as fairness, transparency, and accountability. Industry stakeholders can also play a role in shaping the ethical landscape of AI by adopting ethical codes of conduct, promoting transparency and accountability in AI development and deployment, and collaborating with other stakeholders to address ethical challenges and concerns.

- **Civil Society Organizations:** Civil society organizations, including advocacy groups, non-profit organizations, and academic institutions, play a crucial role in advocating for the ethical development and deployment of AI technologies. They provide independent oversight and accountability mechanisms, monitor AI technologies for potential ethical risks and challenges, and advocate for policies and practices that promote fairness, transparency, and accountability in AI development and deployment. Civil society organizations also play a role in raising awareness and educating the public about the ethical implications of AI technologies, empowering individuals and communities to engage in informed decision-making and advocacy.

- **Affected Communities:** Affected communities, including individuals, groups, and communities that are directly impacted by AI technologies, play a crucial role in shaping the ethical development and deployment of AI technologies. They provide valuable insights into the potential social, economic, and cultural impacts of AI technologies, and their perspectives, needs, and concerns should be taken into account in the design, development, and deployment of AI technologies. Affected communities also have a right to participate in decision-making processes that affect them and to have their voices heard in discussions about the ethical implications of AI technologies.

2. Strategies for Collaborating Among Stakeholders:

- **Engage in Multistakeholder Dialogue:** Foster open and inclusive multistakeholder dialogue and collaboration among diverse stakeholders to discuss ethical challenges and opportunities in AI development and deployment. Create platforms and forums for stakeholders to share their perspectives, exchange best practices, and collaborate on solutions to ethical dilemmas and challenges.

- **Establish Ethical Guidelines and Standards:** Collaborate with stakeholders to develop and implement ethical guidelines and standards for AI development and deployment. Ensure that these guidelines and standards reflect the perspectives, needs, and concerns of diverse stakeholders and are aligned with ethical values and principles such as fairness, transparency, and accountability.

- **Promote Transparency and Accountability:** Promote transparency and accountability in AI development and deployment by sharing information about AI technologies, including algorithms, data sources, and decision-making processes, with stakeholders and affected communities. Establish mechanisms for monitoring and evaluating the performance of AI technologies and for holding stakeholders accountable for adhering to ethical guidelines and standards.

- **Build Capacity and Awareness:** Build capacity and awareness among stakeholders and affected communities about the ethical implications of AI technologies. Provide training, education, and resources to help stakeholders understand and address ethical challenges and dilemmas in AI development and deployment. Empower affected communities to participate in decision-making processes and advocate for their interests and rights.

- **Foster Collaboration Across Sectors:** Foster collaboration and cooperation across different sectors, including government, industry, academia, and civil society, to address ethical challenges and promote ethical AI development and deployment. Establish partnerships and collaborative initiatives that bring together stakeholders with diverse expertise and perspectives to work together on common goals and objectives.

Chapter 14
Mitigating Algorithmic Bias:

In the era of artificial intelligence (AI), algorithmic bias has emerged as a significant concern, impacting various facets of society, from employment and healthcare to criminal justice and financial services. Algorithmic bias refers to the systematic and unfair discrimination present in AI algorithms, leading to biased outcomes that disproportionately affect certain groups or individuals based on factors such as race, gender, ethnicity, or socioeconomic status. Mitigating algorithmic bias is crucial for ensuring fairness, equity, and justice in AI systems and preventing the perpetuation of societal inequalities.

Chapter 14 delves into the complexities of algorithmic bias, exploring its origins, manifestations, and consequences across different domains. It examines the challenges of detecting and addressing algorithmic bias, as well as the strategies and best practices for mitigating bias in AI algorithms. By understanding the root causes of algorithmic bias and implementing effective mitigation strategies, stakeholders can work towards developing AI systems that are more equitable, transparent, and accountable. Through collaborative efforts and ongoing dialogue, we can strive to build a future where AI technologies promote fairness and inclusivity for all.

Understanding Algorithmic Bias and its Implications

In the realm of artificial intelligence (AI), algorithmic bias has emerged as a critical issue with far-reaching implications. Algorithmic bias refers to systematic errors or unfairness present in

AI algorithms, leading to biased outcomes that disproportionately affect certain groups or individuals based on factors such as race, gender, ethnicity, or socioeconomic status. This bias can manifest in various AI applications, including hiring algorithms, predictive policing systems, loan approval algorithms, and healthcare diagnostics tools, among others. Understanding algorithmic bias and its implications is essential for ensuring that AI technologies are developed and deployed in ways that promote fairness, equity, and justice.

1. Origins and Types of Algorithmic Bias:

Algorithmic bias can arise from various sources, including biased training data, biased algorithm design, biased input features, and biased decision-making processes. Biased training data occurs when AI algorithms are trained on data that reflects historical biases or disparities present in society, leading to the perpetuation of existing inequalities. Biased algorithm design occurs when AI algorithms are designed or optimized in ways that systematically favor certain groups or individuals over others. Biased input features occur when AI algorithms use features or variables that are correlated with protected characteristics such as race or gender, leading to discriminatory outcomes. Biased decision-making processes occur when AI algorithms make decisions based on flawed or incomplete information, leading to unfair or unjust outcomes.

There are several types of algorithmic bias, including:

Selection Bias: Occurs when the training data used to train an AI algorithm is not representative of the population it is intended to serve, leading to biased outcomes.

Occurs when the sample used to collect data for training an AI algorithm is not representative of the population it is intended to serve, leading to biased outcomes.

Measurement Bias: Occurs when the variables or features used to train an AI algorithm are biased or inaccurate, leading to biased outcomes.

Aggregation Bias: Occurs when the process of aggregating data or making decisions based on multiple sources of information introduces bias, leading to biased outcomes.

2. Implications of Algorithmic Bias:

Algorithmic bias has significant implications for individuals, communities, and society as a whole. Some of the key implications of algorithmic bias include:

- **Reinforcement of Inequities:** Algorithmic bias can perpetuate existing inequalities and disparities present in society, reinforcing systemic biases and discrimination against marginalized or underrepresented groups.

- **Unfair Treatment:** Algorithmic bias can result in unfair or discriminatory treatment of individuals based on protected characteristics such as race, gender, ethnicity, or socioeconomic status, leading to violations of civil rights and human dignity.

- **Loss of Trust:** Algorithmic bias can erode trust in AI technologies and institutions that use them, leading to skepticism, mistrust, and disengagement among affected individuals and communities.

- **Harm and Injustice:** Algorithmic bias can cause harm and injustice to individuals and communities by denying them opportunities, resources, or services based on biased or inaccurate assessments, leading to negative consequences for their well-being and quality of life.

3. Detecting and Addressing Algorithmic Bias:

Detecting and addressing algorithmic bias is crucial for mitigating its negative impacts and promoting fairness, equity, and justice in AI systems. Several approaches can be used to detect and address algorithmic bias, including:

- **Data Auditing:** Conducting audits of training data to identify biases and disparities present in the data, such as underrepresentation or misclassification of certain groups.
- **Algorithmic Fairness**: Incorporating fairness constraints into the design and development of AI algorithms to ensure that they produce equitable outcomes for all individuals and groups, regardless of protected characteristics.
- **Bias Mitigation:** Implementing techniques to mitigate bias in AI algorithms, such as reweighting training data, adjusting decision thresholds, or using adversarial training to reduce discrimination against certain groups.
- **Transparency and Explainability:** Enhancing transparency and explainability in AI algorithms to enable stakeholders to understand how decisions are made and to identify potential sources of bias or discrimination.
- **Diverse and Inclusive Teams:** Building diverse and inclusive teams of AI developers, researchers, and stakeholders to bring different perspectives, experiences, and expertise to the design and development process, reducing the risk of bias and discrimination.

4. Best Practices for Mitigating Algorithmic Bias:

To effectively mitigate algorithmic bias, organizations and stakeholders can adopt several best practices, including:

- **Data Diversity:** Ensure that training data used to train AI algorithms is diverse, representative, and inclusive of all relevant groups and populations, minimizing the risk of biased outcomes.

- **Bias Awareness:** Raise awareness among AI developers, researchers, and stakeholders about the potential sources and impacts of algorithmic bias, fostering a culture of bias awareness and accountability.

- **Ethical Guidelines:** Develop and implement ethical guidelines and standards for AI development and deployment that prioritize fairness, transparency, and accountability, and adhere to legal and regulatory requirements.

- **Algorithmic Impact Assessment:** Conduct algorithmic impact assessments to evaluate the potential social, ethical, and human rights impacts of AI technologies, and to identify and address biases and disparities in AI systems.

- **Community Engagement:** Engage with affected communities and stakeholders to understand their perspectives, needs, and concerns regarding algorithmic bias, and to incorporate their feedback into the design and development of AI technologies.

Techniques for Detecting and Mitigating Bias in AI Algorithms

As artificial intelligence (AI) technologies become increasingly integrated into various aspects of society, ensuring that these systems are free from bias and discrimination is paramount. Bias in AI algorithms can lead to unfair, inequitable, and harmful outcomes, disproportionately affecting certain groups or individuals based on characteristics such as race, gender, ethnicity, or socioeconomic status. Detecting and mitigating bias in AI algorithms is crucial for promoting fairness, transparency, and accountability in AI systems.

In this exploration, we delve into techniques for detecting and mitigating bias in AI algorithms, examining both proactive measures to prevent bias during development and reactive approaches to address bias in existing systems.

1. Detecting Bias in AI Algorithms:

Detecting bias in AI algorithms is the first step towards mitigating its impact and promoting fairness in AI systems. Several techniques can be employed to detect bias in AI algorithms, including:

- **Data Auditing:** Conducting audits of training data to identify biases and disparities present in the data. This may involve analyzing the demographic composition of the training data, examining the distribution of labels or outcomes across different groups, and assessing the representativeness of the data with respect to the target population.

- **Algorithmic Fairness Metrics:** Using algorithmic fairness metrics to quantify and measure the degree of bias present in AI algorithms. These metrics assess various aspects of fairness, such as group fairness (ensuring that outcomes are equitable across different demographic groups), individual fairness (ensuring that similar individuals receive similar outcomes), and disparate impact (assessing the adverse impact of algorithms on protected groups).

- **Fairness-aware Machine Learning:** Incorporating fairness constraints into the design and development of AI algorithms to ensure that they produce equitable outcomes for all individuals and groups. This may involve modifying the learning objectives or optimization criteria to explicitly account for fairness considerations, such as minimizing disparate impact or maximizing individual fairness.

- **Fairness Testing:** Conducting fairness testing to evaluate the performance of AI algorithms across different demographic groups and identify instances of bias or discrimination. This may involve using synthetic data generation techniques to simulate diverse populations and assessing the algorithm's performance on these synthetic datasets.

- **Interpretable Models:** Using interpretable models or model-agnostic techniques to explain the decisions made by AI algorithms and identify potential sources of bias. This may involve visualizing feature importance or decision boundaries, conducting sensitivity analyses to assess the impact of individual features on model predictions, and examining model outputs for signs of bias or discrimination.

2. Mitigating Bias in AI Algorithms:

Mitigating bias in AI algorithms requires proactive measures to prevent bias during development and reactive approaches to address bias in existing systems. Several techniques can be employed to mitigate bias in AI algorithms, including:

- **Data Preprocessing:** Preprocessing training data to mitigate biases and disparities present in the data. This may involve techniques such as data augmentation, data resampling, or data balancing to ensure that the training data is representative and inclusive of all relevant groups and populations.

- **Feature Engineering:** Engineering features or variables that are less correlated with protected characteristics such as race or gender, reducing the risk of bias in AI algorithms. This may involve removing or de-biasing sensitive features from the input data, or creating new features that capture relevant information without introducing bias.

- **Algorithmic Fairness Constraints:** Incorporating fairness constraints into the optimization process to ensure that AI algorithms produce equitable outcomes. This may involve modifying the learning objectives or optimization criteria to explicitly penalize biased behavior and encourage fairness in model predictions.

- **Bias Mitigation Techniques:** Implementing techniques to mitigate bias in AI algorithms, such as reweighting training data, adjusting decision thresholds, or using adversarial training to reduce discrimination against certain groups. These techniques aim to mitigate bias by correcting for disparities in the training data or by making the algorithm more robust to biases present in the data.

- **Human-in-the-Loop Approaches:** Incorporating human judgment and oversight into the decision-making process to identify and correct biased predictions made by AI algorithms. This may involve providing explanations or justifications for algorithmic decisions, allowing human reviewers to intervene in cases of suspected bias, and incorporating feedback from affected stakeholders into the model refinement process.

3. Best Practices for Bias Detection and Mitigation:

To effectively detect and mitigate bias in AI algorithms, organizations and stakeholders can adopt several best practices, including:

- **Diverse and Inclusive Data Collection:** Ensure that training data used to train AI algorithms is diverse, representative, and inclusive of all relevant groups and populations, minimizing the risk of biased outcomes.

- **Algorithmic Transparency and Explainability:** Enhance transparency and explainability in AI algorithms to enable stakeholders to understand how decisions are made and to identify potential sources of bias or discrimination.

- **Ethical Guidelines and Standards:** Develop and implement ethical guidelines and standards for AI development and deployment that prioritize fairness, transparency, and accountability, and adhere to legal and regulatory requirements.

- **Continuous Monitoring and Evaluation:** Continuously monitor and evaluate the performance of AI algorithms in practice to assess their impact on ethical values and principles, and to identify and address biases and disparities in AI systems.

Case Studies Addressing Bias in Real-world AI Applications

Real-world AI applications are increasingly pervasive, from hiring algorithms and predictive policing systems to loan approval algorithms and healthcare diagnostics tools. However, these applications are not immune to bias, which can lead to unfair, inequitable, and harmful outcomes for individuals and communities. In this exploration, we delve into case studies of real-world AI applications where bias has been detected and addressed, examining the challenges faced, the strategies employed, and the lessons learned in mitigating bias and promoting fairness in AI systems.

1. Case Study 1: Bias in Hiring Algorithms:

Hiring algorithms are used by many organizations to streamline the recruitment process and identify potential candidates for job opportunities. However, these algorithms can inadvertently perpetuate biases present in historical hiring practices, leading to discriminatory outcomes based on factors such as race, gender, or socioeconomic status. In one case study, a large tech company discovered that its hiring algorithm was systematically favoring male candidates over female candidates for technical roles. Upon investigation, it was found that the algorithm was trained on historical hiring data, which contained biases against women in technical roles. To address this bias, the company implemented several strategies, including:

- **Data Auditing:** Conducting audits of training data to identify biases and disparities present in the data, such as underrepresentation or misclassification of certain groups.

- **Algorithmic Fairness Constraints:** Incorporating fairness constraints into the optimization process to ensure that the algorithm produces equitable outcomes for all individuals and groups.

- **Bias Mitigation Techniques:** Implementing techniques to mitigate bias in the algorithm, such as reweighting training data or adjusting decision thresholds.

2. Case Study 2: Bias in Predictive Policing Systems:

Predictive policing systems use AI algorithms to analyze historical crime data and predict future crime hotspots, with the goal of allocating police resources more effectively. However, these systems have been criticized for perpetuating biases and disparities in law enforcement practices, leading to over-policing of certain communities and the disproportionate targeting of racial minorities. In one case study, a city police department implemented a predictive policing system that was found to disproportionately target low-income neighborhoods and communities of color. To address this bias, the police department took several actions, including:

- **Algorithmic Transparency and Explainability** Enhancing transparency and explainability in the predictive policing system to enable stakeholders to understand how decisions are made and to identify potential sources of bias or discrimination.

- **Community Engagement:** Engaging with affected communities and stakeholders to understand their perspectives, needs, and concerns regarding the predictive policing system, and to incorporate their feedback into the decision-making process.

- **Bias Awareness Training:** Providing training and education to law enforcement officers and stakeholders about the potential sources and impacts of bias in predictive policing systems, fostering a culture of bias awareness and accountability.

3. Case Study 3: Bias in Healthcare Diagnostics Tools:

Healthcare diagnostics tools use AI algorithms to analyze medical data and assist healthcare providers in diagnosing diseases and recommending treatment options. However, these tools can be susceptible to bias, leading to disparities in healthcare outcomes for different patient populations. In one case study, a medical imaging company developed an AI-powered diagnostics tool for detecting skin cancer from dermatology images. However, the tool was found to perform poorly on images of darker-skinned patients, leading to misdiagnoses and delayed treatment for these patients. To address this bias, the company implemented several strategies, including:

- **Data Diversity:** Ensuring that training data used to train the diagnostics tool is diverse, representative, and inclusive of all relevant patient populations.

- **Algorithmic Fairness Constraints:** Incorporating fairness constraints into the optimization process to ensure that the tool produces equitable outcomes for patients of all skin tones.

- **Bias Mitigation Techniques:** Implementing techniques to mitigate bias in the tool, such as retraining the algorithm on more diverse data or using adversarial training to reduce bias against darker-skinned patients.

By implementing these strategies, the company was able to improve the performance of its diagnostics tool for all patient populations and promote fairness in healthcare diagnostics

Promoting Diversity and Inclusivity in AI Research and Development

Diversity and inclusivity are essential principles in the field of artificial intelligence (AI) research and development. As AI technologies become increasingly integrated into various aspects of society, it is imperative that the development and deployment of these technologies reflect the diversity of the communities they serve and are inclusive of all individuals, regardless of race, gender, ethnicity, or socioeconomic status. Promoting diversity and inclusivity in AI research and development not only fosters innovation and creativity but also ensures that AI technologies are developed and used in ways that promote fairness, transparency, and accountability. In this exploration, we delve into the importance of diversity and inclusivity in AI research and development, examine the challenges and barriers to achieving these goals, and explore strategies and best practices for promoting diversity and inclusivity in the field.

1. Importance of Diversity and Inclusivity in AI Research and Development:

Diversity and inclusivity bring a multitude of benefits to AI research and development, including:

- **Broader Perspectives and Insights:** Diverse teams bring together individuals with a wide range of backgrounds, experiences, and perspectives, enabling them to approach problems from different angles and generate innovative solutions.

- **Enhanced Creativity and Innovation:** Inclusive environments foster creativity and innovation by creating spaces where all individuals feel valued, respected, and empowered to contribute their unique skills and talents.

- **Better Problem-Solving and Decision-Making:** Inclusive teams are better equipped to identify and address potential biases, blind spots, and ethical concerns in AI technologies, leading to more robust and equitable solutions.

- **Increased Trust and Acceptance:** AI technologies developed by diverse and inclusive teams are more likely to be trusted and accepted by diverse communities, leading to greater adoption and impact in real-world settings.

  Overall, promoting diversity and inclusivity in AI research and development is not only a matter of social justice but also a strategic imperative for advancing the field and ensuring that AI technologies benefit all members of society.

2. Challenges and Barriers to Diversity and Inclusivity:

Despite the importance of diversity and inclusivity, the field of AI research and development faces several challenges and barriers to achieving these goals, including:

- **Underrepresentation of Marginalized Groups:** Women, racial and ethnic minorities, individuals with disabilities, and other marginalized groups are often underrepresented in the field of AI, particularly in leadership positions and decision-making roles.

- **Bias and Discrimination:** Bias and discrimination can create hostile or unwelcoming environments for individuals from underrepresented groups, leading to feelings of exclusion, imposter syndrome, and attrition.

- **Lack of Access to Resources:** Individuals from underrepresented groups may face barriers to accessing educational opportunities, mentorship programs, research funding, and professional networks, limiting their participation and advancement in the field.

- **Cultural and Structural Barriers:** Cultural norms, organizational practices, and institutional policies may perpetuate inequities and disparities in AI research and development, creating barriers to entry and advancement for individuals from underrepresented groups.

   Addressing these challenges and barriers requires concerted efforts and sustained commitment from individuals, organizations, and stakeholders across the AI ecosystem.

3. Strategies for Promoting Diversity and Inclusivity:

Promoting diversity and inclusivity in AI research and development requires a multifaceted approach that addresses structural, cultural, and systemic barriers. Several strategies and best practices can help promote diversity and inclusivity in the field, including:

- **Pipeline Programs and Outreach:** Implementing pipeline programs and outreach initiatives to engage and support individuals from underrepresented groups at all stages of the educational and career pipeline, from K-12 education to graduate studies and professional development.

- **Diverse Hiring Practices:** Implementing diverse hiring practices that prioritize equity, inclusion, and belonging, such as establishing diverse hiring committees, using inclusive language in job postings, and actively recruiting candidates from underrepresented groups.

- **Inclusive Organizational Culture:** Creating inclusive organizational cultures that value diversity, equity, and inclusion, and foster a sense of belonging and psychological safety for all employees. This may involve implementing diversity training programs, establishing affinity groups and support networks, and promoting inclusive leadership practices.

- **Mentorship and Sponsorship Programs:** Establishing mentorship and sponsorship programs that pair individuals from underrepresented groups with senior leaders and mentors who can provide guidance, support, and advocacy for their career advancement.

- **Research Funding and Resources:** Allocating research funding and resources to support projects and initiatives led by individuals from underrepresented groups, and to address research topics and questions that are relevant to diverse communities and perspectives.

By implementing these strategies and best practices, organizations and stakeholders can work together to create more diverse, inclusive, and equitable environments in AI research and development.

Strategies for Ensuring Fairness and Equity in AI Deployment

As artificial intelligence (AI) technologies continue to proliferate across various sectors, ensuring that these systems promote fairness and equity is crucial. AI algorithms have the potential to perpetuate or exacerbate existing biases and disparities, leading to discriminatory outcomes that disproportionately affect certain groups or individuals. To mitigate these risks and promote fairness and equity in AI deployment, organizations must implement robust strategies that address bias, discrimination, and ethical considerations throughout the development and deployment lifecycle. In this exploration, we delve into comprehensive strategies for ensuring fairness and equity in AI deployment, examining key principles, challenges, and best practices in promoting ethical AI.

1. Algorithmic Fairness Assessment:

Algorithmic fairness assessment involves evaluating AI algorithms to identify and mitigate potential biases and discriminatory outcomes. This process encompasses several steps, including:

- **Bias Identification:** Analyzing training data, model outputs, and decision-making processes to identify potential sources of bias, such as underrepresentation or misclassification of certain groups.

- **Fairness Metrics:** Defining and measuring fairness using appropriate metrics and evaluation criteria, such as group fairness, individual fairness, and disparate impact analysis.

- **Bias Mitigation Techniques:** Implementing techniques to mitigate bias in AI algorithms, such as reweighting training data, adjusting decision thresholds, or using adversarial training to reduce discrimination against certain groups.

By conducting algorithmic fairness assessments, organizations can proactively identify and address biases in AI algorithms before deployment, promoting fairness and equity in their systems.

2. Diverse and Representative Data:

Diverse and representative data are essential for training AI algorithms that generalize well and produce equitable outcomes for all individuals and groups. Organizations should prioritize:

- **Data Collection and Curation:** Ensuring that training data is collected from diverse sources and populations, representing the full spectrum of demographic, cultural, and socioeconomic characteristics.

- **Data Preprocessing:** Preprocessing training data to mitigate biases and disparities, such as removing sensitive attributes or balancing the distribution of classes to prevent overrepresentation or underrepresentation.

- **Data Augmentation:** Augmenting training data using synthetic data generation techniques to increase diversity and representativeness, particularly in cases where certain groups are underrepresented.

By leveraging diverse and representative data, organizations can train AI algorithms that are more robust, generalizable, and equitable in their deployment.

3. Transparency and Explainability:

Transparency and explainability are essential for fostering trust, accountability, and understanding in AI deployment. Organizations should prioritize:

- **Model Transparency:** Providing clear documentation and explanations of AI models, including their architecture, input features, decision-making processes, and potential limitations.

- **Explainable AI Techniques:** Using interpretable models or model-agnostic techniques to explain the decisions made by AI algorithms and identify potential sources of bias or discrimination.

- **User-Facing Explanations:** Providing explanations or justifications for AI-driven decisions to end-users, stakeholders, and affected communities, enabling them to understand and assess the fairness of AI systems.

By prioritizing transparency and explainability, organizations can empower stakeholders to engage with AI systems more effectively and hold them accountable for their impact on fairness and equity.

4. User Feedback Mechanisms:

Incorporating user feedback mechanisms into AI deployment processes enables organizations to gather insights, identify issues, and address concerns related to fairness and equity. This involves:

- **Feedback Loops:** Establishing feedback loops that allow users and affected communities to provide input, report issues, and suggest improvements related to the fairness and equity of AI systems.

- **Community Engagement:** Engaging with diverse stakeholders, including community groups, advocacy organizations, and affected individuals, to solicit feedback, address concerns, and co-design solutions that promote fairness and equity.

- **Ethical Advisory Boards:** Establishing ethical advisory boards or review panels comprised of diverse experts and stakeholders to provide guidance, oversight, and recommendations on ethical considerations in AI deployment.

By incorporating user feedback mechanisms, organizations can foster transparency, accountability, and continuous improvement in their AI deployment practices.

5. Continuous Monitoring and Evaluation:

Continuous monitoring and evaluation are essential for assessing the performance, impact, and effectiveness of AI systems in real-world settings. This involves:

- **Performance Metrics:** Defining and tracking performance metrics related to fairness, equity, and ethical considerations, such as bias scores, demographic parity, and error rates across different demographic groups.

- **Ethical Impact Assessments:** Conducting regular assessments to evaluate the social, ethical, and human rights implications of AI systems, and to identify and address any unintended consequences or disparities.

- **Algorithmic Audits:** Conducting periodic audits and reviews of AI systems by independent third parties to assess their compliance with ethical standards, legal requirements, and organizational policies.

By continuously monitoring and evaluating AI systems, organizations can identify emerging issues, make informed

decisions, and take timely corrective actions to ensure fairness and equity in deployment.

www.ingramcontent.com/pod-product-compliance
Lightning Source LLC
LaVergne TN
LVHW061551070526
838199LV00077B/6990